A FRAMEWORK FOR VALUE MANAGEMENT PRACTICE

A FRAMEWORK FOR VALUE MANAGEMENT PRACTICE

Michel Thiry

Library of Congress Cataloging-in-Publication Data

Thiry, Michel
Value management practice / Michel Thiry
     p.   cm.
Includes bibliographical references
ISBN: 1–880410–14–1 (pbk.)
Industrial project management. I. Title.
HD69.P75T466   1997
658.4'04--dc21   97–12912
                                                   CIP

Book Team
Editor-in-Chief: James S. Pennypacker
Editor, Book Division: Toni D. Knott
Acquisitions Editor: Bobby R. Hensley
Book Designer: Michelle Owen
Cover Design by: Allison Boone
Production Coordinator: Mark S. Parker

PMI books are available at special quantity discounts to use as premiums and sales promotions, or for use in corporate training programs. For more information, please write to the Business Manager, PMI Publication Division, 40 Colonial Square, Sylva, NC 28779. Or contact your local bookstore.

The paper used in this book complies with the Permanent Paper Standard issued by the National Information Standards Organization (Z39.48—1984).

10   9   8   7   6   5   4   3   2   1

DEDICATION

I would like to dedicate this book to Robert P. Charette, project engineer and certified value specialist, who has been my mentor during my value management learning, and to other value managers around the world, who have willingly shared their knowledge with me. In particular, I would like to mention Howard Ellegant from the United States, Francine Constantineau from Canada, Dudley Fowler from Ireland, Matthew Locke from the United Kingdom, and Guy Brun from France.

I also would like to thank all of the people at Project Management Institute, Society of Value Engineers International, Canadian Value Analysis Society, Association française pour l'analyse de la valeur (AFAV), and the Institute of Value Management, who have openly shared and discussed their ideas with me—and continue to do so—enabling persons such as myself to develop further.

Table of Contents

List of Figures

Preface

For many years, the terms **value analysis** (VA) and **value engineering** (VE) have been used alternately. There still exists disagreement concerning their exact meanings; they depend, for the most part, upon the country or the national association using them. In this book, "value analysis" includes both value analysis and value engineering, in accordance with the new EN 1325-1 European standard. The consensus today is to use **value management** to describe the integrated widespread application of value techniques. It encompasses function analysis, value engineering, value analysis, value control (validation), and other value techniques. Value management also involves the skills and knowledge needed to manage the value process by applying the correct tools and techniques at the appropriate time, allowing the greatest benefit to the project. It involves planning and coordination of the process and training of the team.

Value management methodology is based on a few determining principles and concepts that are the framework upon which value practitioners build and add substance through constant sharing of ideas. This book has been inspired by the work and experiences of leading value practitioners. It aims to provide a scope of current practices, from which new value practitioners may extract principles, concepts, tools, and techniques to develop individual value management practices. Therefore, the book will require updating as value management continues to evolve.

In the **first chapter**, the book provides the background needed to understand the origins of value management. The **second chapter** comprises a description of value management's guiding principles and concepts, and the **third chapter** describes tools and techniques that can be used to achieve the objectives of a value study. The **fourth chapter** covers value integration.

The **Appendix** section has been organized into three topics—**Value Management Associations, WWW Sites,** and **Value Analysis Forms**—for keeping current. The **References** section at the end of the book includes magazine articles, standards, and books, as well as a **Videography**, including visual documents. Books have been selected for their contribution to the value management body of knowledge, and articles are either milestones of value management or new trends.

CHAPTER I

History of
Value Management

THEORY AND TECHNIQUES

Value analysis/engineering is not a new concept; its origin dates to World War II. Its success was challenged at times, yet flexibility and continued improvements have enabled value analysis and value engineering to overcome roadblocks with remarkable results. As the old saying goes, *the proof of the pudding is in the eating.*

We will explore the theory and techniques of value management through the value professionals who have contributed to value engineering and value analysis growth and recognition throughout the years.

1940 to 1960: More for Less

Value analysis/engineering was first developed by Lawrence D. Miles, an electrical engineer with General Electric (GE), now universally known as the "father of value engineering." When World War II broke, material shortages began occurring, and electrical components that once were plentiful were committed to strategic applications. A product that had been produced easily in the past had to be redeveloped using different materials. The function remained the same, but the method of providing that function had to be changed. Miles, who had often in the past been dissatisfied with the high cost of many of GE's projects, realized that many times when circumstances force people to do things differently—altering a design or using a different material, for example—the result is superior performance combined with reduced cost.

At first, the functional approach was related to decreasing cost; subsequently, it was expanded to evaluate the overall value of the product. The program developed by Miles was called value analysis/engineering, and its purpose was to analyze the cost necessary to achieve the required function without jeopardizing the reliability of the product.

The first value analysis seminars at General Electric were conducted in 1952. A multidisciplinary team was organized to involve the key decision-makers, and the team concept was an instant success. In the late fifties, Miles structured value engineering through a job plan concept and published *Techniques of Value Analysis and Engineering* (2d ed. 1972).

1960 to 1980: Opening New Paths

In 1965 Carlos Fallon, then director of purchasing research at RCA, worked on a matrix analysis approach to decision-making. This system offered the basic benefits of mathematics-oriented analysis yet was relatively easy to use and understand; he called it "Combinex" (Fallon 1965, vol. XXI).

In the early sixties Charles W. Bytheway, an engineer with Sperry Rand's Univac Division, developed the function analysis systems technique (FAST) diagram (1985). FAST is a structure aimed at organizing functions in a logical and orderly manner, and it may have been inspired by the concepts of work breakdown structure (WBS) and critical path method (CPM) that were introduced and very popular in project management at the time.

Many value engineers developed individual versions of function analysis systems technique diagramming; two of them are more notable. Wayne Ruggles, then executive vice president of Value Analysis Inc., developed—with the help of J.K. Foulkes and John Groothuis—what is now known as the "technically oriented FAST."

Thomas J. Snodgrass, president of Value Standards Inc. and a professor at the University of Wisconsin, devised a market research-based technique to compare a function's "worth to the customer" with its actual cost and, with Theodore C. Fowler, developed the "customer-oriented FAST" (Snodgrass and Kasi 1986; Snodgrass and Fowler 1972, sec. 9.0).

1980 to Present: Towards Value Management

In 1986 Thomas Cook simplified and modified Snodgrass' data-based methodology in order to assess value mismatches with a customer-oriented point of view (Cook 1986, v. XXI, 145–56). This and other developments of the sixties and eighties paved the way for value analysis and value engineering's expansion from manufactured product analysis and construction into new fields.

In the eighties basic value engineering methodology was well described by Larry Zimmerman and Alphonse Dell'Isola (Zimmerman and Hart 1982; Dell'Isola 1988). Only in the late eighties and early nineties did the rise of new methods enable value practitioners to implement value analysis techniques at a much earlier stage and to integrate them into the project management process, thereby creating a true management tool. Some of those new methods are the *Cahier des charges fonctionnel*

(CdCF) developed in France (Brun 1993; Tassinari 1985); strategic value planning (SVP) by Stephen Kirk (1993), modern value engineering (MVE) by Howard Ellegant (Summer 1993), and customer-oriented value engineering (COVE) by John Bryant in the United States (1986); and value management by John Kelly and Steven Male in the United Kingdom (1993).

Outlook: Integration

More and more value practitioners are questioning the traditional forty-hour value engineering workshop and evolving towards the process known as value management that integrates throughout the entire project life-cycle. Many practitioners also are developing techniques to use value management much earlier in the project. This evolution has opened new possibilities for value integration into project management.

New fields continue to respond to value management techniques, such as reengineering (Hays 1995), organizational management, change management, concurrent engineering, and others. Value concepts also are integrated into known processes, such as project management (PM) (Thiry 1996), total quality management (TQM) (Fuerstenberg 1994; Ellegant Avril 1993), and design to cost (DTC) (Ruskin 1995), for example. The concept of value is so universal that the only obstacle to furthering value management development is the inhibition of the value practitioner. Who knows who will be the next Miles or Bytheway?

Value Management Expansion

The United States Department of Defense's Navy Bureau of Ships established the first governmental value program in 1954. The method was to be applied at the engineering stage, which brought about a change in name from value analysis to value engineering. In late 1958, the first group of value engineers united under the name of the Society of American Value Engineers (SAVE). Due to SAVE's steady lobbying for the use of value analysis and value engineering, governmental agencies adopted the methodology for their projects. In the early sixties, the Department of Defense proclaimed that its subcontractors would use value engineering, and in 1973 General Service Administration did the same regarding design and construction management contracts.

Following the Navy's lead, the United States Army and Air Force began visiting their suppliers, attempting to motivate them to launch value engineering programs in order to help reduce defense costs. Success was an embarrassing moderate to nothing. It was clear that suppliers were being penalized rather than rewarded for suggesting value engineering savings because their fees or profits were calculated according to the cost of the project. In 1963 the Armed Services Procurement Regulation (ASPR) Committee mandated that value engineering incentives would be included in contracts thus allowing percentage sharing by the contractor and the supplier on approved savings proposals, known as value engineering change proposals (VECP).

On February 10, 1996, the United States Office of Federal Procurement Policy Act (41 U.S.C. 401 et seq.) was amended to include Section 4306 which states the following: "Each executive agency shall establish and maintain cost-effective value engineering procedures and processes."

In Europe, more and more governmental organizations are requiring function-based specifications (for example, see CdCF in France) in their public bidding systems and value management in their projects. The European Community Programme for Innovation and Technology Transfer (SPRINT) has been promoting value analysis since 1988 as one of the innovative management techniques strengthening companies' innovative capacity and competitiveness. It has published a widely distributed booklet entitled "Better Management Through Value Analysis" in the nine official languages of the community.

Soon after the Society for American Value Engineers was founded, value engineering began to spread around the world. In 1965 the Society of Japanese Value Engineers was founded, and, later, value engineering societies were formed in Italy (Associazione italiana per l'analisis del valore), Germany (Verein Deutcher Ingenieure), France in 1978 (Association française pour l'analyse de la valeur), England (Institute of Value Management), South Korea, Saudi Arabia, Kuwait, Australia, Denmark (Danish Technological Institute), India (Society of Indian Value Management), Taiwan and South Africa in the eighties, and Hungary (Society of Hungarian Value Analysis) and Canada in 1993 (Canadian Society of Value Analysis). In 1992 a group of value societies formed the World Federation of Value Societies (WFVS).

Establishing Value Analysis/Value Engineering Certification and Standards

In 1970 the General Services Administration (GSA) recommended the establishment of a value engineering program for its construction projects, and in 1973 the GSA Public Building Services required that value engineering studies be included in its construction contracts. General Services Administration asked the Society of American Value Engineers (SAVE) to develop a certification program for value practitioners; the status of **certified value specialist (CVS)** was established by SAVE as a standard, recognizing competence in the field of value engineering (SAVE 1993). Today, many such programs exist around the world.

In the United States, the SAVE International has three levels of certification: associate value specialist (AVS), value management practitioner (VMP), and certified value specialist (CVS). The associate value specialist represents the basic level and recognizes the ability to participate in a workshop and help facilitate it. Value management practitioner is an intermediate level aimed at managers or coordinators of value management programs that do not need the facilitator certification. Certified value specialist is the highest level of certification and recognizes a seasoned value management practitioner.

The Institute of Value Management of Australia recognizes four levels of membership: associate member, member, member practitioner, and fellow. In France, the Association française pour l'analyse de la valeur recognizes three categories of certification. Category I is targeted for the teaching of value analysis and comprises two levels of certification; category II is aimed at practitioners and has four levels, the two higher levels being animateur (CANV) and expert (CEXV). Category III focuses on value analysis program managers and/or sponsors. In Germany, the Zentrum Wertanalyse offers three levels of certification: value analyst, value analyst coordinator, and value analyst teacher. India and Japan recognize certified value specialist certification. India and Japan recognize SAVE International certified value specialist certification, Japan also has a value engineering leader certification for junior level personnel which is recognized by the Japanese Government. In Ireland, Forbairt certified the first Irish value analysts in 1996, based on the German model.

South Africa's Value Engineering and Management Society of South Africa currently recognizes three levels of accreditation. Value analysis/value engineering/value management practitioner (VA/VE/VM) is the first level; value engineering/value analysis/value management facilitator (VE/VA/VM), the second level, requires some value management facilitation experience; and the third level, value analysis/value engineering/value management trainer (VA/VE/VM) requires training experience. In the United Kingdom, the Institute of Value Management currently acknowledges three levels of qualification: certificated value practitioner (CVP), capable of leading value management workshops and studies; certificated value educationalist (CVE), skilled in teaching value management; and certificated value manager (CVM), capable of conducting value studies and control value management programs.

Germany developed the first value standard in 1973: DIN 69 910 on "Wertanalyse"(value analysis). From 1985 to the early nineties, Association française de normalisation (AFNOR) standards X50-100, 150, 151, 152, and 153 on value analysis were introduced in France. In 1987 the Bureau of Indian Standards set up standard IS:11810-1986 on value engineering. The American Society for Testing Materials (ASTM) developed a standard in 1995, and a European standard is being developed by the Commission europeenne de normalisation (CEN).

CHAPTER II

Theory

Value

If a design has not changed in 18 years, the product is either excellent or management has failed to improve it.

Larry Zimmerman
American Value Specialist

First, we will introduce the concept of "value"; we will then investigate how value is managed. Value is a very subjective concept; it has different meanings for different people. A consumer will regard it as the "best buy," a manufacturer will consider it the "lowest cost," and a designer will view it as the "highest functionality." Value does not stand alone: "In other words, value is a concept of time, people, subject, and circumstances, not just the subject alone" (Snodgrass and Kasi 1986, 257). A very interesting concept was related by a customer in a survey and reported in Robert Tassinari's book, *Le rapport qualité/prix* (1985): "Value is a combination of dream and concern. Dream is the idea one has of a product; concern is when you get the product and wonder if you've had your money's worth."

The concept generally accepted by value managers is that value is a ratio of quality and cost; however, quality and cost can vary widely, according to the point of view.

What is Value?

Since Miles' time, value has evolved from a simple quality/cost ratio to a more customer-oriented notion.

Value increases when the satisfaction of the
Customer's need augments and the expenditure of
resources diminishes.

(Tassinari 1985, 37)

Customer value is a measure of relativity that consists of a balance between quality and resources. Quality is the capability to respond to the customer's needs, and resources are the global overall resources needed to fulfill that need.

Often, when setting up a project, there is a mismatch between the customer's intent and his capability. The value system's objective will be to find or recreate the balance between these two elements in order for the project to be a success. Every step of the way, the project team must aim for that balance between what is expected, what is needed, and what resources are available to produce it.

In integrated value management, value is always customer-oriented. An easy way to remember customer value is as follows:

$$\text{Customer Value} = \textbf{NOT MORE} = \frac{\textbf{N}\text{eeds} + \textbf{O}\text{bjectives} + \textbf{T}\text{argets}}{\textbf{M}\text{aximum } \textbf{O}\text{verall } \textbf{R}\text{esources } \textbf{E}\text{xpended}}$$

What is Good Value?

The goal in value management is not merely to reduce costs but to balance performance with cost. "Good value" is achieved when balance is obtained between quality and resources. Although value is a subjective concept, it can be measured.

Quality can be defined as the ratio of what is offered versus what is expected; if the offered is equal to or greater than the expected, quality responds to the need. Resources should be balanced between what is available and what is required. If what is available is equal to or greater than what is required, the need can be fulfilled. This concept can be illustrated as follows.

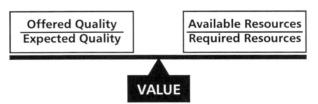

Figure II-1   The Value Concept

Following the above concept, value can be attributed the following characteristics:

Worst Value	$= Q < 1$	$R \geq 1$
Low Value	$= Q = 1$	$R > 1$
Good Value	$= Q = 1$	$R = 1$
	$Q > 1$	$R > 1$
Best Value	$= Q > 1$	$R = 1$

If **R<1,** the project cannot occur or the product cannot be obtained. "Poor value" usually is caused by a lack of an adequate level of the following characteristics.

Individuals	Organization	Technology	Environment
Leadership	Objectives	Products	Funding
Habits	Structure	Processes	Timing
Attitudes	Planning	Skills	Politics
Adaptability	Communication	Expertise	Regulations

These inadequacies often result in ambiguous objectives, misleading information, hasty decisions based on false assumptions, lack of sufficient funds, and resistance to change.

Types of Values

There are many types of value, and all of them must be considered in a value study. Depending on the client's objectives, they will vary in importance, and more energy should be spent on optimizing those considered most important, while the less important ones might not be considered at all.

Use Value—The amount of current resources expended to realize a finished product that **performs as it was intended.**

Esteem Value—The amount of current resources a user is willing to expend for functions attributable to **pleasing rather than performing;** e.g., prestige, appearance, and so on.

Exchange Value—The amount of current resources for which a **product can be traded**. It is also called **worth**, as the minimal equivalent value considered.

Cost Value—The amount of current resources expended to achieve a function **measured in dollars.**

Function Value—The **relationship** of function **worth** to function **cost**.

Value Management

William Peña—in the excellent book, *Problem Seeking* (Peña, Parshall, and K. Kelly 1987)—establishes five steps for architectural programming: (1) establish **goals**; (2) collect and analyze **facts**; (3) uncover and test **concepts**; (4) determine **needs**; and (5) state the **problem**.

Value management—a term first used in 1974 by the General Services Administration—much like architectural programming, addresses goals and problems. Value management can exist only when a goal needs to be achieved or a problem needs to be solved; when there is no goal or problem, there is no need to improve value. Therefore, it is important for the value team to establish goals and state the problem.

Value management consists of the integration of proven and structured problem-solving techniques known as **value methodology**). They are implemented by a **multidisciplinary team** under the guidance of a knowledgeable **value practitioner** "to seek out the best functional balance between the cost, reliability, and performance of a product or project" (Zimmerman and Hart 1982).

Seeking balance in today's constantly changing environment involves an openness of mind and an adaptation capacity that can be considered an "authentic" learning process. This is true not only of individuals but also of organizations. In his book, *The Fifth Discipline* (1990), Peter Senge lists eleven "laws" that govern the "learning organization":

1. Today's problems come from yesterday's "solutions."
2. The harder you push, the harder the system pushes back.
3. Behavior grows better before it grows worst.
4. The easy way out usually leads back in.
5. The cure can be worse than the disease.
6. Faster is slower.
7. Cause and effect are not closely related in time and space.
8. Small changes can produce big results, but the areas of highest leverage are often the least obvious.
9. You can have your cake and eat it, too, but not all at once.
10. Dividing an elephant in half does not produce two small elephants.
11. There is no blame.

Failure to observe one or more of these laws creates an unbalanced situation that has led many organizations to downfall. As more value managers become aware of organizational deficiency, potentially leading to the cause of the problem they are trying to solve, understanding of these laws becomes fundamental.

The value study is graphically described in Figure II-2.

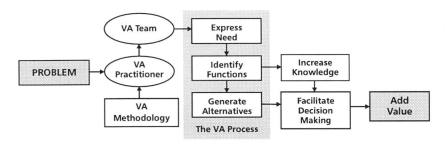

Figure II-2   The Value Process

Function

Function is the basis of value management; function analysis is a fundamental step in any value study. We will see how a need, objective, target, or concept can be described in terms of function and what function means.

What is a Function?

A function is a concept by which value management describes a need in terms of its expected performance rather than its expected solution. This concept enables the value team to generate creative alternatives that are not based on paradigm.

The need generates the product; function is the link between them. If the process is consistent, the resulting product should correspond to the need (see Figure II-3).

Definition of functions by breakdown of need   **Definition of product by association of functions**

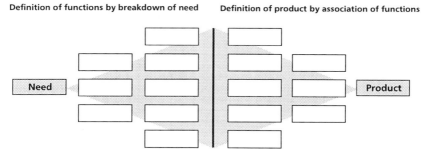

Figure II-3   The Need-Function-Product Process

A product is the result of an action aimed at fulfilling the customer's needs. Products can be objects, services, systems, buildings, processes, software, or any other solution to perform a function.

Referring to need, Fallon stated: "If excessive is generally bad, desirable is generally good; to ignore this fundamental distinction can lead, during a VA [value analysis] study, to dismiss the desirable, believing it excessive" (1977). This brings us to reconsider the definition of customer need in a broader sense that includes desires as well. John Bryant includes desires in the concept of value and describes customer value as follows: wants + needs/resources (1986).

In order to establish customer-oriented value, one should understand that the need, expressed through its functions, is totally independent of technical solutions. Therefore, we can reasonably state that the customer's need is usually quite stable, even if the technical solutions needed to fulfill it vary or evolve rapidly. If one bears in mind the satisfaction of the basic needs and manages to abstract the technical solutions, even a client that seemingly changes his mind all the time is much easier to handle.

Functions usually are described using a verb and a measurable noun (e.g. chair = support weight). There are reasons for this method: abstraction from technical solutions, accuracy of the statement, broken down concept, "in extenso" description, clarified perception, easier consensus, and stimulated thought processes.

Functions have a few basic characteristics:
- Functions are use- or performance-oriented.
Chair is a solution, support weight is a performance or use.
- A product can have several functions.
An office chair can support weight and allow movement.
- Functions are totally independent of solutions.
Support weight can be accomplished with many different solutions: chair, stool, sofa, and so on.
- Each function of the same product is independent.
A wheelchair should offer the best solution to support weight as well as the best solution to carry an individual.

Types of Functions

There are different types of functions. Primary or basic functions are those functions for which the product exists and that guarantee its performance. They can be divided into use functions (needs) and esteem functions (wants). For example, a chair must support weight, but it also should indicate status. Primary functions should be customer-oriented, dictated by the client's wants and needs.

Supporting functions, also called secondary functions, are not secondary at all. They correspond to a complementary need that must be satisfied just as much as the basic need; e.g., a chair must not only support weight but also provide comfort. The supporting function is as important as the primary function, even if it is not essential to the product's performance.

Technical functions result from the design or the fabrication of the product, e.g., the "resist lateral effort" function of a chair. Customers often are not even aware of their existence, although they may be essential to the performance. Technical functions should never be considered in a function analysis that is not specifically directed at analyzing a design or an existing product.

Constraints are all the functions created by codes, regulations, standards, site (in construction projects), technology limitations, market, and so on. These constraints usually are very specific; for example: "Endure 2,000 strikes of a fifty pound weight at an interval of ten seconds with less than 0.01 inches of deflection in the seat structure." In customer terms, this translates to "exceed warranty." It is very important for the value management practitioner to recognize and uproot the "false constraints" that result from a lack of determination to find a solution to a problem.

Unnecessary functions are all the functions that could be eliminated without affecting the product's performance; for example, the "fact" that a chair must have four legs. Unnecessary functions usually are the result of honest wrong beliefs and assumptions or the perpetuation of obsolete requirements.

The Team

> *Working independently, the resolution [of a problem]*
> *by one discipline becomes the problem of another.*

J. J. Kaufman
American Value Specialist

The use of a multidisciplinary group is essential for creating completeness and consensus on proposed alternatives. Including participants from all levels and activity of a project will ease communications and prevent distortion of facts.

Composition

Traditionally, value studies have been conducted by means of a forty-hour workshop with a team of "experts" external to the project. This method is not appropriate to integrated value management, though, except under very specific conditions. In general, the "guerrilla team" principle also is not suitable in today's organizational environment. As Peter Senge stated (1990): "People don't resist change, they resist being changed."

Howard Ellegant maintains that by using a peer review team on a value engineering workshop, you create an "adversarial relationship between the design team and the VE [value engineering] study team" (Summer 1993). He also says: "The very people who have to approve and implement the recommendations have no ownership of them and no stake in a positive outcome!"

Jerry Kaufman lists the following advantages of an "in-house" task value team (1992): easier implementation because of "buy in" of proposals; absence of adversarial confrontation with "outside" sources; development of professional respect; and compression of implementation time. He concludes that outside teams often are perceived as "venture capitalists" by internal resources.

It is essential that the participants in the workshop include representatives of all parties involved with the project concept, development, execution, and use because needs and objectives should be defined and evaluated from every possible angle, and proposals should be endorsed by every participant.

A complete value management team includes those who "own" the problem or opportunity (supplier); those responsible for its resolution (supplier's experts and consultants); and those who are impacted by its decision (buyer). An example of a list of participants for typical project workshops is presented in Figure II-4. Actual team composition will vary according to the type and size of the project.

A well-balanced value team should be able to address all of the "ilities" of a project, namely: producibility (constructibility), usability, reliability, maintainability, availability, operability, flexibility, social acceptability, and affordability (Ireland 1991, II-2–5).

Failure to fulfill the above requirements will greatly affect the outcome of any value study.

Tasks and Responsibilities

Each participant in the value team has responsibilities and tasks to accomplish.

LEADER

The leader's first task is to conduct the workshop, but he or she also has the responsibility of preparing the team adequately by securing all the appropriate data and warrant that it complies with the standards. The leader also needs to ensure that all members of the team have an adequate knowledge of value management and understand the job plan. The leader also is responsible for identifying the study's objectives, ensuring adherence to the job plan, and following up on recommendations.

The leader must be responsible, open minded, humble, and able to synthesize. This person will exercise leadership on three levels: functional (procedure and organization), expertise (content and competence), and social (atmosphere and influence).

PARTICIPANTS

The number of participants should be limited; usually there are five to twelve. They should be of equivalent hierarchical degree, well motivated, and they should accept and endorse the value management principles during their participation in the study.

CUSTOMER/CLIENT

The customer must be convinced of the methodology, accept having to "open his books" for the study, and discuss freely his true needs and objectives.

The Job Plan

The value engineering/value analysis job plan is "an organized approach to the conduct of a value study," according to the Society of American Value Engineers' certification examination guide (1993). The structure of value analysis is based on the job plan, which is universal in its approach. It has been successfully applied to manufacturing, systems processes,

	Manufactured Product	Construction	Services
Supplier (Internal)	Marketing Finance Engineering Purchasing Operations and Processes Sales	Feasibility Development Project Management Design Management Construction Management Facilities Management	Marketing Finance Research and Development Staff Management Line Management Service Staff
Buyer	Consumer	User	Beneficiary
Consultants (External)	Process Consultants Technical Consultants Buyer	Design Consultants Cost/Schedule Technical Consultants Constructibility	External Consultants
Value Team Leader			

Figure II-4   List of Function Analysis Workshop Participants in Typical Projects

construction projects, health care facilities, software development, and others. The job plan is the framework against which all value analysis actions are taken.

Why a Job Plan?

There are many good reasons to follow a job plan; following are eight of them:

1. To obtain better results through a systematic approach.
2. To use the allotted time in the most efficient way.
3. To force participants to go beyond set standards.
4. To emphasize performance over solutions, through function analysis.
5. To identify high optimization potential areas.
6. To allow everything to be questioned in a partnering environment.
7. To base recommendations and results on measurable data.
8. To convince stakeholders to endorse the method for reasons one through seven.

Participants in a value study should be cautioned about the tendency to disregard the step-by-step approach of the job plan. The study would eventually catch the obvious value mismatches or high cost elements, but it would overlook most of the expected results of a well-conducted workshop.

Job Plans

There are a number of standardized value management job plans, depending on the country and/or organization; every value manager develops his own variation of the job plan. The job plan should be perceived as a foundation upon which every specific value study is developed, depending on the project to be tackled.

The author promotes the following basic steps of the value management process: (1) analysis of needs/statement of problem (information/preparation and function analysis; (2) development of solutions (speculation/creativity); (3) selection of solutions (analysis/evaluation and study/development and options appraisal; and (4) implementation of solutions (recommendation/follow-up). Some of these phases should be part of a workshop while some are accomplished outside the work environment.

The following job plans have been standardized by value associations around the world and are part of official standards.

TRADITIONAL : FIVE-PHASE

Value practitioners traditionally follow a standard five-phase job plan derived from Miles' early fifties seven-phase job plan that was designed to study existing manufactured products and try to improve them. Variations of this job plan exist, but they basically consist of subdividing the five phases into sub-phases or naming the phases differently. The standard job plan includes the following (Zimmerman and Hart 1982):

- **Information** phase, during which all participants are presented the project and pertaining documents, and function analysis is performed.
- **Creative** phase, when ideas are generated in a brainstorming session.
- **Judgment** phase, at which time ideas are evaluated by the team according to their merit.
- **Development** phase, when ideas kept from phase three are developed into proposals.
- **Recommendation** phase, at which time proposals are presented to the client for implementation.

AMERICAN SOCIETY FOR TESTING MATERIALS: SIX-PHASE

A more integrated approach destined to design or reengineer products, processes, or projects is gaining acceptance. Consequently, more emphasis has been put on function analysis—which begins to appear between phases one and two as a phase in its own right—and on the follow-up of the proposal's implementation. This evolution is reflected in the recent American Society for Testing Materials' standard job plan presented below (1995), as well as in the Department of Defense and the General Services Administration's job plans (Zimmerman and Hart 1982, 35).

- **Information** phase, during which all participants are presented the project, owner's requirements, and pertinent data.
- **Function Analysis** phase, at which time function analysis is performed and cost/worth ratios are calculated.
- **Creative** phase, or when ideas are generated through creative thinking.
- **Evaluation** phase; the time to rank ideas and evaluate alternatives.
- **Development** phase, when proposed alternatives are developed, and life-cycle costs are estimated.
- **Presentation** phase, when findings are summarized and presented to the client for implementation.

ASSOCIATION FRANÇAISE DE NORMALISATION (AFNOR): SEVEN-PHASE

In France, the Association française de normalisation (AFNOR) has standardized a seven-phase job plan that puts more emphasis on "functional expression of need" and "function analysis" and integrates pre-workshop and post-workshop activities (1985, NF X 50–153). It is outlined as follows:

PREPARATION
1. Orientation of activity
2. Data gathering

NEEDS ANALYSIS
3. Function and cost analysis

SOLUTIONS ANALYSIS
4. Search of ideas and solution leads
5. Study and evaluation of solutions

RESULT IMPLEMENTATION
6. Anticipated results, presentation of proposals
7. Follow-up of implementation

HER MAJESTY'S TREASURY CENTRAL UNIT ON PROCUREMENT: SEVEN PHASE

In the United Kingdom, Her Majesty's Treasury recommends an integrated value management process, consisting of a series of reviews throughout the project. Each review is based on seven key steps: (1) orientation, a time to identify what is to be achieved, the key project requirements, priorities, and desirable characteristics; (2) information, when relevant data about client needs, wants, values, costs, risks, time-scale, and other project restraints is gathered; (3) speculation, a time for generating alternative options to achieve client needs within stated constraints; (4) evaluation of the alternative options identified during the speculation step; (5) development of the most promising options and their more detailed appraisal; (6) recommendation for action; and (7) implementation and feedback, a time to examine how the recommendations were implemented to provide lessons for future projects.

Dertsche Industriell Normen (DIN) Standard: Six Phase

German's DIN standard relies on a six-step work schedule: (1) project preparation, (2) analysis of object situation, (3) description of ideal status, (4) development of solution ideas, (5) determination of solutions, and (6) implementation of solutions. The process is iterative and guided by a constant reassessment of progress achieved towards project objectives.

Bureau of Indian Standards: Ten Phase

In India, the value engineering standard was established in 1986 and relies on a ten-step job plan: (1) introduction and orientation, (2) project selection and detailed seminar, (3) information, (4) function analysis, (5) creative phase, (6) analysis, (7) evaluation, (8) recommendation and presentation, (9) implementation, and (10) feedback and collateral applications. The plan includes training and awareness in phases one and two.

Objectives of Each Phase

Before any value management workshop can begin, the value management study objectives should be discussed with the client. The way a workshop is conducted may vary enormously depending on when and why it is conducted.

The objectives of each phase also may vary from one job plan to another. Thus, we will examine basic objectives that should always be present because they lay the foundation for any value management workshop.

In the following section, we have followed the American Society for Testing Materials' job plan. It is basic but considers function analysis as a distinct phase; therefore, we consider function analysis as one of the most important phases in a value analysis/value engineering study.

Information/Presentation Phase

This phase includes a presentation of the project by the client, the project manager, and/or the design team. Depending on the phase of the project during which the workshop takes place, the client sets his requirements (needs and objectives), the project manager or the client explains the project parameters (constraints and available resources), and the design team presents the design and estimated costs. The costs should be presented in elemental format and models. Life-cycle costing should be included if available.

The goal is to clearly identify the needs and objectives of the client and make them unequivocal for every participant in the project and to identify potential optimization elements/areas for further study.

Function Analysis Phase

Function analysis is extended to the degree required to better understand the project or a part of the project. Depending on the phase of the project during which the workshop takes place, the function analysis will be more or less elaborate. At the early stages of the project, all options are still open, and function analysis becomes an integral part of the strategic planning and feasibility process. When conducted early in the project, it can be used effectively to determine the scope and setting of the project, which will create a baseline for change management.

The purpose is to create a "virtual" model of the project in terms of the functions it should perform and to eliminate all trace of technical solution.

Speculation/Creativity Phase

This phase is the shortest of the workshop; using creative thinking, hundreds of ideas can be generated in a few hours. The ideas are not discussed or judged; later phases will be devoted to thoughtful evaluation and careful development.

The goal is to generate enough ideas/alternatives that will meet the requirements of the client.

Analysis/Evaluation Phase

Ideas are discussed only to the degree required to understand what is proposed. Impractical alternatives are eliminated, and experiences are shared to identify advantages and disadvantages. Ideas are then rated and ranked according to all relevant considerations, using one of several evaluation techniques.

The target is to evaluate all ideas/alternatives in a timely manner and to select the ones with the highest value potential for the development phase.

Study/Development Phase

Chosen alternatives are measured and developed individually or in small groups by team members in consultation with others. For each alternative, a **value management proposal** is written, including support to implementation, such as: life-cycle cost estimates, conformity to functions, impact on schedule, technical merit, risk evaluation, and other appropriate considerations.

The objective is to document each of the selected proposals in measurable terms with enough detail to convince the team to recommend them or eliminate them.

Recommendation/Presentation Phase

The team classifies the proposals as to functional and/or technical merit and time to implement and then summarizes the findings. An oral presentation of results is made to the stakeholders on the final half-day of the workshop, and a draft report of the proposals and summaries can be presented to the project manager in order to start implementation procedures immediately without further delay.

The object of the presentation is—for the client, project manager, and designers—to adopt the proposals in view of their implementation. The report that follows should clearly establish the results of the study and confirm the meeting of the initial objectives.

In **value management integration**, the job plan is basically the same except that it is integrated into the project and extended over a longer period. Pre-workshop and post-workshop activities—orientation and follow up—are given more emphasis since the value practitioner is involved earlier and must support implementation and value control. These two latter phases will be examined in more detail in Chapter IV.

For detailed methodology of the value engineering job plan, see also Dell'Isola and Zimmerman (Dell'Isola 1988, 14, fig. 2-2; Zimmerman and Hart 1982, chap. 3) . Although their work is primarily directed towards the traditional forty-hour workshop, it is beneficial.

Where and When to Use Value Management

Every time a new product or project is being planned, or an existing product or project needs improvement, the application of value management should be considered. More specifically, when a product does not sell or generates complaints from customers, or when new markets need to be explored, value management is profitable. When a project is not evolving according to plan, or when one of the project parameters or objectives is not achieved, value management techniques are applied to bring it back on track.

Ideally, value management should be implemented in the very early stages of a project when a commitment has not yet been made. This enables value to be used to its greatest potential: to clearly identify the expected performance and functions of the product/project. If this is not possible, it is still feasible to use value management very effectively at any stage of the planning or development phases of a project.

Any size product or project is suitable to a value study; only the extent of the study and the size of the team will vary. As long as the value, function, multidisciplinary team, and job plan concepts are present, it is value management. During his Module II Seminar, held in Montreal in 1995, John Bryant said, "Even if you don't call it Value Management, it doesn't matter; as long as you apply the Value methodology principles, it still is Value Management."

CHAPTER 3

The Management of Value

Preparation

*Large amounts of highly organized material are
required to expand the range of possibilities before a
new and useful combination of ideas can be generated.*

William Peña
American Architect

William Peña's five steps of architectural programming (see p. 9) should be conducted by the value team during the preparation/information phase and the function analysis phase (Peña, Parshall, and K. Kelly 1987). Steps one (establish goals) and two (collect and analyze facts) are part of the preparation phase, and step three (uncover and test concepts) pertains to the information phase. The function analysis process answers step four (determine needs), and step five (state the problem) is the output of the functional analysis process (see Figure II-3).

Integrated value management is an "open, circular system" in which the output from one phase becomes the input of the next and feeds back to the preceding phases. Therefore, steps one through five will be iterated many times throughout the project life-cycle in order to reassess customer value. In practice, steps may be taken in a different order, or they may occur at the same time.

Identification of the Need

*Total Quality Management is doing the job right;
Value Management is doing the right job.*

J. J. Kaufman
American Value Specialist

Process control has always been the basis for total quality management-based project management, and it has been demonstrated that good process control will aid in performing the job correctly. Today, though, clients are asking for more than a job done properly. Value management is designed to identify the customer's needs in order to do the right job; when combined with project management, it will do the right job right.

The first step in identifying customer value is to understand the concept of need. The need should not be mistaken with the way it is expressed; need is created by a lack, or a feeling of a lack. Usually, because we are greatly influenced by advertising, we express our need through a product. The "need" we experience in that manner is often far removed from the actual need we have to fulfill, and the product we obtain fills the void only very temporarily. A good example of this is the case of the Ninja Turtles that were suddenly replaced by the Power Rangers, or Walt Disney's Aladdin and Jasmine that were shoved aside by Pocahontas and John Smith.

Clients are not different from children in that they "need" the new product that just came out, be it a new computer program or the world's tallest building or the latest high-technology machine. **The need should generate the product and not vice versa**.

When identifying customer needs, even accomplished value practitioners have a tendency to concentrate on cost reduction and forget other client objectives. Value management can help the client have his cake and eat it too, if the value team focuses on needs rather than solely on cost reduction.

The value study leader must take the time to identify the client's needs and wants and ask him appropriate questions about the project, such as: "What is your problem?" "Why is this a problem?" "Why is a solution necessary?" The value practitioner should be both the translator of the customer's vision and the challenger of his strategy.

Dr. Stephen Kirk suggests holding "an interactive workshop [where] project expectations are brought out, explored and documented" (1994). He continues:

> These expectations may involve schedule, image,
> flexibility, functionality, technical systems performance,
> budget adherence, or any other issue which may shape
> the direction of the project. The relative importance
> between these competing values are explored,
> prioritized and documented with the owner.
>
> Through collaborative workshops with the owner, a
> clear understanding, documentation and prioritization
> of the above competing values are realized for the
> project. These expectations and goals are explored and

discussed in the workshop. Specific owner definitions
of each competing value are developed.

CUSTOMER-ORIENTED VALUE

Historically, Value studies have concentrated on "use"
functions [...] however, when attempting to improve
the Value of products, "sell" functions become vitally
important. [...] "Value Mismatch" occurs when the
producer places a different emphasis or degree of
importance on use or sell functions than does the
purchaser.

John Bryant
American Value Specialist

As we have seen in the section on value in chapter two, value has different meanings for different people. Often, when setting up a project, there is a mismatch between the customer's intent and capability; the value study's objective is to find, or recreate, the balance between these two elements in order for the project to be a success. Every step of the way, the value team must always aim for that balance between what is expected, what resources are available to produce it, and what is needed.

The customer's perceived quality is often far removed from the quantified, measurable quality of the supplier and his expert consultants. Many examples exist of "perfect" products that were a fiasco because of "misperception" of what the customer really wanted. This type of value mismatch occurs when the supplier and the customer do not have the same definition of the performance of a product, or when they have the same definition but don't place the same relative importance on its functions.

Customer needs should be regarded as a system, one in which each element has an influence on the rest. It is only by contemplating the whole, not an individual part, that you can understand the system. All these elements are to be listed and addressed to create a cohesive picture of the customer's quality expectations and resource capabilities. It will then, and only then, be possible to offer the customer a project/product that will match or exceed his expectations while considering his ability to afford it.

The basis of customer-oriented value management is to identify the design criteria and the areas of improvement that are meaningful in the customer's perception of value.

The **customer value** concept must be present throughout the study, guiding every decision, from information to function identification, evaluation of ideas, and development of proposals.

The Value Management Team

The reasonable man adapts himself to the world,
while the unreasonable one persists in trying to adapt
the world to himself. Therefore, all progress depends
on the unreasonable man.

George Bernard Shaw

As we have seen earlier, the value management team should be composed of representatives of all the participants in a project. Since we want a diversified value team, goals and agendas will not be the same for all participants, and since we also want the team to deliver original solutions, one should not expect team members to be reasonable. We will examine each team member's role and/or influence.

IDENTIFYING INFLUENCES

The mood of the value workshop is usually set during the first half-hour. It is, therefore, very important for participants in a value management workshop to understand the influence external stakeholders can have on the outcome of the study and the project process. The team has to be balanced, and participants must be well prepared in order to avoid pitfalls during and after the value study.

STAKEHOLDERS

Stakeholders usually do not participate in the workshop, but they are the true customers, the ones who have much to gain and/or lose. Consumers are considered customers only if the study focuses on the design of a product that is backed by marketing studies. In the case of an existing product, consumer comments must have been collected prior to the workshop.

The client usually is a company; therefore, it is difficult to identify your true customer. A good rule of thumb is to identify the person responsible for "signing the check," as this person usually is the one to convince of the cost effectiveness of the study.

Another important stakeholder is the project manager, the one responsible for the success of the project and who will therefore be interested in any method that facilitates the work or increases control over the project.

The operations and maintenance (facilities) manager and the user are the ones who will be most aware of the project/product's performance in the end. Therefore, they will be very interested in the long-term (life-cycle) performance of the product.

Finally the chief executive officer or board of directors will usually be the entity to create the "esteem functions." They are the ones that care more about image and not so much about cost.

In understanding how each stakeholder respectively influences the project, the value management team can very accurately determine the interests at stake and develop a value system that will enable them to establish priorities and find the best customer value, be it cost, esteem, life-cycle, or success of the project.

PARTICIPANTS

Value management workshop results are optimized when all participants are convinced that the methodology works. This may mean holding an information session prior to the workshop to ensure that everyone involved in the study has the same level of understanding of the process and its expected results.

The team should be well balanced between technical and functional experts as well as between planning, execution, and operations personnel. All fields covered by the project should be acknowledged.

It is not recommended that management people be included as participants in the workshop unless they are very familiar with value management and respect its rules. Managers usually will have the most at stake during a value study. They also have a tendency to unwillingly overwhelm other participants and take the floor, especially during the creativity phase where parity of opinions is essential. If managers must be integrated into the workshop, it is best to include them in the judgment or development phases when creativity is at its minimum.

PERSON IN CHARGE OF IMPLEMENTATION

It is beneficial to remember that implementation of proposals is the ultimate measure of success of the value study; it also is the most difficult task to achieve since the value team does not have the responsibility of implementation. Therefore, it is very important to identify the person who will be in charge of implementation as early as possible in the study; one of the goals of the value study is to help that person buy-in the recommendations of the value study. The value management team should be aware that one way to accomplish this is to let this person know how his work will be eased and how results will be improved by value management.

TEAM PREPARATION

As we have stated earlier, it is important that all the team participants possess the same basic level of understanding of the value management methodology. Therefore, it might be important to provide a basic training session in value management before the workshop actually takes place. Furthermore, team participants should receive all pertinent information regarding the study to be undertaken prior to the workshop in order to become familiar with the project beforehand. This will focus energies during the information phase and enable participants to clarify ambiguous issues or objectives to be discussed later. The author uses a "briefing pack" that also lists objectives, constraints, participants, proposed agenda, and others to accomplish this.

Each member of the value team is to spend a specified period of time examining the background information of the project. Usually, one-half day to two days per person is allowed for this task, depending on the size and magnitude of the project. Familiarization can be done independently.

TEAM WORK

> *By design and by talent, we were a team of specialists,*
> *and like a team of specialists in any field, our*
> *performance depended both on individual excellence*
> *and how well we worked together. None of us had to*
> *strain to understand that we had to complement each*
> *other's specialties; it was simply a fact.*

Bill Russell
Boston Celtics Player, 1956–69

Considering that a good value management multidisciplinary team is composed of specialists, understanding the principles of team work and accepting them are key elements to the success of the value study. Team development involves four basic characteristics: a common vision, which is developed through the information phase; a viable structure, provided by the job plan; a reward system, achieved through "changing the world" and implementing it; and good team leadership, which is established by a competent value team leader.

The basic principle of teamwork is to be able to relate to others; every participant is aware of her own personality (pros and cons) and tries to understand other teammates' values, feelings, and points of view. A few aspects that are important when participating in a team include procedures and respect for them, sticking to the subject, and content, including making your interventions short and to the point, always trying to make the issue progress, accepting the team's decisions, listening to understand, expressing your feelings, and asking for clarification if needed. Other important aspects are action, involving making your own experience and resources known, volunteering for tasks to be accomplished, taking initiatives and implementing them, and actively inputting evaluation; and social, including being positive in all your interactions, being a team player, being cheerful and helpful, and collaborating.

The structure of the value management job plan is designed in such a way that the team spirit builds and becomes contagious; even conflicting individuals have a difficult time negatively influencing the group if the team sticks to the job plan.

Creative Thinking

Imagination is more important than knowledge.

Albert Einstein

Habits, paradigms, preconceptions; these attitudes are an important part of everyday life and very useful, too, but they are the worst enemies of creativity. But why use creativity techniques in value management? There are many reasons, such as to overcome our natural resistance to change, to favor the structured expression of innovative ideas, to avoid "stillborn" ideas by deferring judgment, to tactfully control overpowering individuals, and to enable shy individuals to express their ideas.

Creativity should not be restricted to the creativity phase; it is a process that also can be very useful in other phases. For example, in the information phase, it assists in defining the problem and evaluating potential benefits of the study. In the function analysis phase, creativity can benefit in generating a list of functions with good descriptions; in the creativity phase, it helps with identifying numerous alternatives to fulfill the functions. Creativity is beneficial in listing criteria by which functions will be judged during the evaluation phase, and it can assist with identifying selling points and possible objections and to find the easiest implementation paths for the proposals during the recommendation phase.

CONCEPTS

In order to come up with one good idea, you must have lots of ideas.

Linus Pauling, Swedish Scientist

As we have seen, the entire value management process benefits from creativity. There are four essential steps involved in creativity: preparation, gestation, enlightenment, and implementation. Also, two basic theories must be applied when performing creativity: the association of ideas and successive use of both sides of the brain.

Association of ideas, in turn, consists of three basic principles: similarity, contiguity, and contrast—principles stated by Aristotle that are still valid. It is important to use both hemispheres of the brain in a consecutive and constructive manner to achieve creativity. The process is divided into two phases: imagination, or creativity, and analysis, or judgment. In value management, creativity and judgment are used alternatively to analyze and solve the problem under study.

Creative thinking relates to "lateral thinking," which consists of exploring new paths of thought instead of pursuing a given path (de Bono 1992). Creative thinking is an open-minded process to which some considerations of lateral thinking can be applied. For example, vertical thinking is selective, lateral thinking is generative; vertical thinking is sequential, while lateral thinking can jump. With vertical thinking, one excludes what is irrelevant; with lateral thinking one welcomes chance intrusions. Vertical thinking follows the most likely paths, and lateral thinking explores the least likely ones.

Some basic rules apply to creative thinking:

1. Write all ideas and comments.
2. Target quantity rather than quality.
3. Exclude criticism; assume that each idea will work.
4. Hold judgment until the evaluation phase.
5. Eliminate "impossible" from your vocabulary.
6. Let your imagination roam free (the craziest ideas are often the most important).
7. Use piggybacking (build on other ideas and comments).
8. Cross-fertilize ideas (associate or modify ideas and comments).
9. Let everybody talk; do not interrupt!
10. Build a friendly competitive atmosphere.

Psychological safety and freedom of speech should be an integral part of any creative session; therefore, it is important that participants be on the same level of authority or that any manager or supervisor who participates in the workshop be very open-minded and trusted by the other team participants.

TECHNIQUES

Before choosing any of the following techniques, the value manager must evaluate the type of project, its stage, objectives, and the composition and background of the team members. Also, techniques can be combined, since the ultimate goal is to form a vast quantity of ideas in a short period of time.

BRAINSTORMING

Brainstorming is a group process which was developed in the seventies by Alex Osborn (1971). It begins with the identification of the problem or leads; the group is then asked to meet as a whole to determine creative solutions to the problem. It is the process that can be applied the most widely in value management.

GORDON TECHNIQUE

This technique consists of a group brainstorm based on general knowledge of the function(s) or broad area of a problem without any specific knowledge of the problem itself. The exact problem is not identified until the leader feels that all possible solutions have been explored.

CHECKLISTS

The goal is to generate ideas from data and collect good ideas accumulated in other similar studies or projects. This technique is very useful if one can identify ideas that have occurred regularly in past studies or projects.

MORPHOLOGICAL ANALYSIS

The idea behind this technique is to divide a problem into its parameters (elements); a model is then developed that lists all the possible combinations that might lead to a solution. Combinations and/or permutations of elements are then "tried" to solve the problem. Usually, one axis is used for the processes, the vertical axis represents design, and the third axis is for technical parameters.

ATTRIBUTE LISTING

Attributes and characteristics of the problem are listed and then the impact of changing one or the other is examined. This technique allows new combinations of characteristics or attributes to solve the problem.

ENVIRONMENT ANALYSIS

This method is used in function analysis, as promoted by the Association française pour l'analyse de la valeur (AFAV). It consists of identifying all external factors that relate to a project or product and listing their impact (in terms of functions) on the project, the project's impact on them, and their impact on each other throughout the existence of the project or product.

In integrated value management, various creativity techniques are used in function identification and in the first value analysis workshop at the early development stage (pre-design). During value control workshops, only brainstorming is used.

The goal always is to find a vast quantity of ideas to work with, whatever the method employed to attain it.

Data Gathering

He who grasps at much holds fast little.

Spanish Proverb

Data gathering is a key phase of any value study. Too little information leads to a partial statement of the problem. The appropriate amount of information should be broad enough in scope to pertain to the whole project but not so broad as to get out of focus. The crux of the information process lies in organizing data for easy assimilation.

The entire value management process is based on the relevance, accuracy, and knowledge of data significant to the project or product under study. Data gathering can, therefore, be divided into three steps: collect, analyze, and communicate data.

COLLECT DATA

First, the team leader should identify all the data needed to successfully conduct the value study while keeping its scope in mind. This person then should collect all data from the different parties involved in the project and identify all missing information. The following questions should be asked: What facts are known? What do you need to know that you don't know? Where or how can information be obtained?

The Project Management Institute lists eight functions for project management that basically cover the main areas of a project: scope, quality, time, cost, human resources, procurement, risk, and communications. Reviewing the five programming steps for each of these project management functions can be a good checklist for possibly missing information. Other functions also must be covered in specific application areas, for example, "safety" in construction management or "security" in information technology.

All collected data and information must be recorded and supported with facts.

ANALYZE DATA

Collected data is then verified and validated. All information—fact or assumption—is documented and sources are identified. Opinions or prejudices are recognized and restricted as much as possible.

Information is consolidated—meaning that it is classified, cross-referenced, and cross-checked—in order to make sure that facts are presented only once (no contradictions), and that the reference is valid. This step should be conducted with the help of the team participants who have the expertise to evaluate specific data and validate it.

COMMUNICATE DATA

Once information is classified and consolidated, the team leader will structure the information into a framework and format data in order to best communicate it to all participants on the team as well as to obtain consensus from the stakeholders. This involves preparing models, graphics, tables, sketches, and so on. Data communicated to the team can include design, estimates, schedules, functional relationships, organizational structure, procurement facts, environment, legal structure, standards and regulations, technical restrictions, and so forth.

The amount of data provided by a client can be staggering. It is the team leader's responsibility to synthesize all information to prevent what Peña calls a "Data Clog," which "causes confusion and prevents clear conclusions. [It] paralyzes the thought processes and a mental block against all information can result" (Peña, Parshall, and K. Kelly 1987).

Peña also states: "One can assimilate any amount of information, as long as it is pertinent, meaningful, and well organized for **effective** use."

Cost Techniques

Cost is a major frame of reference used to assess the value of the products we acquire. This value might be in terms of the quantity, quality, aesthetics, image or other criteria. In the comparison of alternatives cost adds the element of objectivity needed to analyze alternatives.

Larry Zimmerman
American Value Specialist

Value practitioners should always remember that **cost is a means, not an end**. Cost techniques can be used in many phases of the study or project; for example, in the information phase, they are useful in identifying potential optimization (life-cycle costing analysis, budgeting, cost models, and so on). During the function analysis phase, these techniques are helpful in allocating function costs and cost/worth while in the evaluation phase, they help to compare alternatives, such as cost/worth models and matrixes. Cost techniques can aid in estimating the cost of alternatives (elemental estimates and life-cycle costing) in the development phases and in communicating potential benefits to the client during the recommendation phase.

This section is intended to show the degree of accuracy required at various stages of design and to show how the cost estimates are transformed into cost models used to relate and compare alternatives. Cost estimates and cost models are communication tools; they also are a standard frame of reference that will give all parties a means to understand the exchange value (worth) received in return for investment dollars. The aim is to have all members of the project team agree on costs.

COST ESTIMATING

Cost estimates can be prepared by the design consultant or by a cost consultant; the value consultant must ensure that costs are accurate. Cost estimates are prepared using different levels of complexity. The type of estimate will vary to correspond to the purpose, complexity, and phase of the project as well as data accuracy and availability.

During the preliminary planning stages of the project, the degree of accuracy of cost estimating usually is conceptual in nature and based on past trends and historical knowledge of similar projects (see 1 and 2). During the conceptual and development stage, costs are based on elements (see 3 and 4). As the project develops, more and more data is generated to detail cost estimates (see 5). Cost units also vary during the project evolution.

1. User costs are based on units of basic function performed. Examples of user costs are cost per bed in a hospital design, cost per gallon of chemical produced, and cost per capita per day for treatment of sewage. User costs are applied to obtain a gross estimate of the total project cost.

2. Spatial cost parameters are used in construction projects; they are based on linear feet, square feet, or cubic feet.

3. Elemental costs are grouped by functional systems and subsystems.

4. Parameter costs frequently are used in the process industry to describe costs for systems and unit operations.

5. Unit costs are the cost of each unit of material or equipment and labor hour used in the project.

Cost estimates form the basis for cost models used in a value study. Zimmerman has organized costs into five orders of complexity: first order costs, or the total cost of the facility; second order costs, a combination of system costs; third order costs, distribution of cost by subsystem; fourth order costs, components and by construction trade; and fifth order costs, detailed estimates based on actual costs (Zimmerman and Hart 1982, chap. 7).

Public Works and Governmental Services Canada (PWGSC) uses a "D to A" classification for building construction projects. It is generic for cost, time, and performance and is specified as follows:

• Class "D" Estimate is based upon a comprehensive statement of requirements in mission terms and an outline of a solution. Such an estimate is strictly an indication of the final project cost and completion date.

• Class "C" Estimate is based upon an outline description of overall scope and siting of the equipment or facility sought. It should be sufficient for making the correct investment decision.

• Class "B" Estimate is based upon data (relative to cost, timing, and production or construction) of quality equivalent to that available following the definition of the major systems and subsystems of the equipment or facility, including an outline of specifications and preliminary drawings and models. This type of estimate should provide for the establishment of a realistic budget and schedule, sufficiently accurate to permit control of a project.

• Class "A" Estimate is based upon a complete description of the equipment or facility sought, such as would exist when the concept design, working drawings, and detailed specifications and other significant conditions of production or construction are available.

It is important to respect these units and complexity parameters in order to optimize the value of the study. The goal of the value study is to attain the greatest value within the allotted time-frame. If too much time is spent on detailing estimates at a stage where the proportion of assumptions is still substantial, less time will be available to increase the value of the project, and proposals will be based on inaccurate data.

ELEMENTAL ESTIMATING

Elemental estimation consists of classifying construction project estimates according to their components (elements). This method was first used in the United Kingdom and was exported to Canada by British Quantity Surveyors and then to the United States. The Canadian Institute of Quantity Surveyors, Royal Architecture Institute of Canada, and the American Institute of Architects have been promoting elemental estimating since the early eighties. In 1993, the American Society for Testing Materials issued Standard E 1557-93, "Standard Classification for Building Elements and Related Sitework—Uniformat II." This standard is now beginning to be recognized as the elemental classification standard.

The concept of elemental estimating is not exclusive to construction; it can be applied to any product. The concept consists of dividing the cost of a project into its components in a hierarchical way, very similar to a function breakdown structure (FBS) or a work breakdown structure (WBS). The advantage is to be able to identify cost allocation very soon in the project and still be able to proceed into more detail as information becomes available. Elemental estimation provides a continuous structure for the design phase of the project for program (brief) specifications, drawings, and cost (Charette and Shooner 1995). Figure III-5 is an example of an "Uniformat II" elemental estimate system.

LIFE-CYCLE COSTING (LCC)

Life-cycle costing was first developed in the United Kingdom in the thirties by Eugene L. Grant and was soon adopted by the Public Services Administration. It was introduced in the United States in the early fifties at Bell's Engineering Economy Department. In 1980, the American Society for Testing Materials issued Standard E 917-89 (revised 1989) on life-cycle costing.

There are many definitions of life-cycle costing. The American Institute of Architects (AIA) defines life-cycle costing as follows (Haviland 1978):

> *Any technique which allows assessment of a given*
> *solution, or choice among solutions, on the basis of*
> *considering all relevant economic consequences over*
> *a given period of time (or life cycle).*

Value management relies on life-cycle costing at every stage of a value management study to evaluate optimization potential or compare alternatives or proposals. Life-cycle costing consists of comparing cost/worth alternates on the same calculation basis by bringing all the costs to a common baseline on two basic principles: the global expenditure of resources and the present value of future expenditures.

GLOBAL RESOURCES

When estimating costs or expenditure of resources, the value team must be aware that—in office building construction, for example—capital or investment costs represent approximately half the life-cycle cost of the project. In order to accurately compare alternates, one must consider all the types of expenditures involved in the project. For example, in a construction project, the following would be considered: initial costs, including soft costs (feasibility and design fees), development/construction costs, and financing costs; useful life costs, involving soft costs (legal and administration fees) and financing, operation, and maintenance costs, as well as taxes; and end-of-life costs, involving salvage value and cyclical alteration/replacement costs.

PRESENT VALUE

The second principle is the "time value of money," and it consists of comparing present and future expenditure of monies on an equivalent basis known as "present value." Some basic economic parameters must be set before entering time value calculations. They include period of study, discount/interest rates, escalation/inflation rates, cyclical renewal periods, taxation provisions, financing methods, and investment criteria (return on investment, pay-back period, and so on).

Economic formulas are the mechanism used to equate the factors of time, interest, present costs, future costs, and annual costs. For ease of use, these formulas have been translated into tables or included in "financial" calculators.

To understand life-cycle costing calculations, two basic concepts are necessary: the concept of compound interest and the concept of discounting, which is the reverse. Discounting is the method used to express costs at any given time on an equivalent basis.

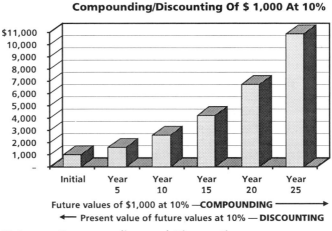

Figure III-1   Compounding and Discounting

The basic formulas for calculating present value (P) and future value (F) are the following, where i represents the interest rate and n, the time period:

$$P = \frac{F}{(1+i)^n} = F(1+i)^{-n} \qquad F = P(1+i)^n$$

As a rule, the present value is always smaller than the equivalent future value. All other formulas for calculating present and future value of uniform series of payments, escalating amounts, future investments, and so on are derived from these two.

Another definition that might be important to remember is the difference between constant and current dollars. Constant dollars are expenses of past or future years expressed in the dollar value of a reference year (present value). Current dollars are the actual dollar value of expenses in the specific year in which they occur.

USING LIFE-CYCLE COSTING

Before proceeding with a life-cycle analysis, it is best to be certain of the validity and availability of cost parameters in regard to the expected accuracy of the results. Using life-cycle analysis as a decision-making tool involves certain steps, such as: identify the problem to be solved; document alternate schemes with background information on technical components and their differences; and establish parameters because life-cycle analyses are impacted by time, cost, and the cost of money. Time involves setting the useful life of the project and each of its major components in order to assess alteration/replacement costs. Cost encompasses the initial costs, useful life costs, and end-of-life costs. The cost of money is considered by setting interest, inflation, and escalation rates.

While life-cycle costing provides an excellent tool to assist in decision-making, its application should be understood to avoid possible pitfalls in its use. Life-cycle costing dollars are constant and, therefore, do not reflect actual budget dollars, estimate dollars, cash-flow dollars, and the obligated amounts for each funding year. The exact point in time when an extra investment will be repaid is sometimes hard to assess. Life-cycle costing is based on assumptions that can change very quickly (return of revenue, interest rates, and escalation). Return on investment rates and pay-back period may vary according to non-economical factors. The estimates are only as good as the background data forming the basis for costs, and the analysis of results is based solely on economic factors.

Final analysis should account for non-economic criteria that have intrinsic benefits that do not lend themselves to finite cost evaluations. The final decision on abstract factors relies heavily on judgment, as **factors such as safety, reliability, operability, and environmental factors, to name a few, may be more important than monetary savings.**

Criteria for making life-cycle analyses include many areas that force decisions using soft numbers that create a margin of error inherent in the life-cycle costing process. However, the order of magnitude of the cost comparison makes life-cycle costing a worthwhile tool. **It is the best tool available for computing order of magnitude comparisons.**

Modeling

Give me a lever long enough and, single-handed, I will lift the world.

Aristotle

Because of the limited time allocated to studies, value management relies on modeling techniques to increase understanding of the project and to communicate complex concepts that would otherwise be difficult to visualize by the client and other participants. Models are a great communication tool and since the value methodology puts a strong emphasis on efficiency, modeling should be part of the value practitioner's vocabulary. Model analysis should be a central part of any integrated value management study. Modeling techniques can be used in many phases of the study or project; for example, they help with identifying potential optimization (cost models, quality, models, and so on) in the information phase. In the function analysis phase modeling techniques can help with function breakdown structure and element/component models, while in the evaluation phase, they aid in comparing alternatives with previous models (cost/worth models). Finally, in the recommendation phase, these techniques help to communicate with the client.

The author uses the following modeling techniques.

COST MODELING

The cost model is a tool used to organize and distribute estimated costs into functional areas that can be easily defined and quantified. Elements of the cost model should relate to a cost estimating system that can be organized easily into functional areas' trade breakdowns.

To construct the cost model, the value team coordinator and/or the estimator on the value team distributes cost by process, trade, system, and other identifiable areas. This helps the value team at the beginning of the study to know where the major costs are to be found (see Figure III-1).

Pareto's Law of Economics indicates that 80 percent of the cost will normally occur in 20 percent of the items being studied. The cost model helps to identify the 80 percent of the project cost. An outline of the high-cost areas of the project is developed at this point so that the costs are well organized when the team meets, and time can be used effectively.

COST MODELS (see Figure III-2 and Figure III-3)

In the early information phase, cost models are based on disciplines involved in the project. For example, in construction those disciplines would include architecture, structure, electrical, mechanical, and landscape; for software development, design, development, testing, and marketing may be involved; and for pharmaceutical, disciplines may include research, pre-clinical testing, clinical testing, governmental approval, and marketing. They usually are presented in the form of a bar chart or a work breakdown structure.

MATRIX COST MODEL (see Figure III-4)

Costs are organized by functional system and subsystem (function breakdown structure) along the vertical axis, and by construction trade or other component breakdown (work breakdown structure) on the horizontal axis. A matrix cost model is especially useful for process plant designs when there is more than one unit process and also when a large complex of component parts is repeated throughout each unit process. The cost matrix can be readily understood and utilized by the designer to analyze cost per process function and cost per trade element. Depending on the project, cost can be reflected with functional quantities. In any case the costs should be organized so that one can equate the cost with an identifiable functional quantity.

FUNCTIONAL COST MODELS

The functional cost model distributes the project costs by functional area. Costs used in the model include two types. The estimated construction cost or the actual cost and the target cost or the worth or target cost is the value engineering team's estimate of the least cost to perform the function. Identifying the project target costs is performed jointly by team members. The worth is the least cost to perform the required function. Projecting a worth on the various cost categories stimulates team members to devise alternative solutions to the original design. Models involving cost play an important part in the value engineering process; for this reason team members with a keen sensitivity to cost should be chosen.

ELEMENTAL COST MODEL (see Figure III-5)

Elemental cost models are a hierarchical representation of the product/project based on its elements. In building construction, they are based on the Uniformat II (or equivalent) American Society for Testing Materials standard. Elemental models can be designed for any type of product/project.

COST/WORTH MODELING (see Figure III-6 and Figure III-7)

Cost/worth models are based on the exchange value. From the list of functions, the team establishes a worth model that can be rendered in a graphical form such as a Gantt diagram (bar chart). Each function's worth is calculated by estimating the lowest expense of resources needed to fulfill the function. The cost is then calculated by estimating the proposed solution or alternative's function expected resource expenditure and comparing it against its worth. This model will be used to identify functions or components for which the team can observe a cost/worth mismatch that justifies its being addressed in the value analysis workshop. A high differential between cost and worth indicates a low value for that function/component.

FUNCTION MODEL

The function breakdown structure (FBS) (see Figure III-15) is the basic output of the function analysis workshop; all other models and conclusions depend upon it. It is the function breakdown structure that will help build a customer-oriented work breakdown structure for the project. On the left, you will find the higher order function (main objective of project). The function breakdown structure will be developed until a function can be related to a measurable component. The function breakdown structure will help share the project function's concept (and value system) with all participants, and it will enable the project manager to quantify the project in terms of cost and time, according to its functionality and expected performance.

QUALITY MODELING

Quality modeling has been developed by Smith, Hinchman & Grylls (SH&G), a Detroit architectural and value management firm. Quality criteria are established with the client and validated with designers in order to obtain consensus. A quality model is then built against which all design alternatives are pondered and judged (see Figure IV-3).

SPACE MODELING (COMPONENT MODEL)

The space model mostly is used in construction projects; it is a graphical representation of the functions/components of a building and their mutual relationship. Areas are calculated according to regulation and client requirements for each function as well as anticipated population. Technical requirements are then added to each component to produce the technical program. Comparable component models can be used in any study.

OTHERS

Models are very useful to the value practitioner. Once the basic principles of modeling are understood, you can create your own models according to the information you want to share. Computer programs like Excel or Lotus are very easy to use and can be very handy tools for building models. In construction projects, for example, it is possible to use a test reference building (TRB), a virtual model derived from the space model, to calculate the worth of the project (Charette 1981).

All of these modeling techniques can be used to the extent dictated by the size and complexity of the project.

MODEL EXAMPLES

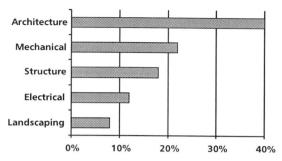

Figure III-2   Bar Chart Cost Model

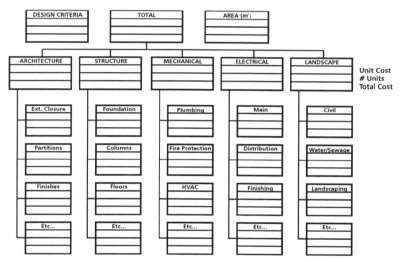

Figure III-3   Hierarchical Cost Model

	ELEMENT / COMPONENT										TOTAL COST OF FUNCTION	
FUNCTION Verb + Noun	Element A		Element B		Element C		Element D		Element E			
	$	%	$	%	$	%	$	%	$	%	$	%
		0%		0%		0%		0%		0%	$0.00	0%
1 Verb + Noun					$0.00		$0.00				$0.00	0.00%
2 Verb + Noun			$0.00				$0.00		$0.00		$0.00	0.00%
3 Verb + Noun	$0.00				$0.00						$0.00	0.00%
4 Verb + Noun	$0.00										$0.00	0.00%
5 Verb + Noun	$0.00		$0.00		$0.00		$0.00				$0.00	0.00%
6 Verb + Noun			$0.00						$0.00		$0.00	0.00%
7 Verb + Noun	$0.00		$0.00								$0.00	0.00%
8 Verb + Noun									$0.00		$0.00	0.00%
9 Verb + Noun			$0.00				$0.00		$0.00		$0.00	0.00%
10 Verb + Noun			$0.00				$0.00				$0.00	0.00%
... Verb + Noun	$0.00				$0.00				$0.00		$0.00	0.00%
TOTAL COST OF ELEMENT												100%

Figure III-4   Matrix Cost Model

TABLE 1: UNIFORMAT II BUILDING ELEMENTAL COST SUMMARY   -   Project:

ELEMENTS LEVEL 2		RATIO	ELEMENT COST			ELEMENT	COST per	% TRADE
	Elements Level 3	QTY/GFA	UM	Quantity	Unit Price	AMOUNT	UNIT GFA	COST
A10	FOUNDATIONS					-	-	
A1010	Standard Foundations				-	-		
A1020	Special Foundations				-	-		
A1030	Slab on Grade				-	-		
A20	BASEMENT CONSTRUCTION					-	-	
A2010	Basement Excavation				-	-		
A2020	Basement Walls				-	-		
B10	SUPERSTRUCTURE					-	-	
B1010	Floor Construction				-	-		
B1020	Roof Construction				-	-		
B20	EXTERIOR CLOSURE					-	-	
B2010	Exterior Walls				-	-		
B2020	Exterior Windows				-	-		
B2030	Exterior Doors				-	-		
B30	ROOFING					-	-	
B3010	Roof Coverings				-	-		
B3020	Roof Openings				-	-		
C10	INTERIOR CONSTRUCTION					-	-	
C1010	Partitions				-	-		
C1020	Interior Doors				-	-		
C1030	Specialities				-	-		
C20	STAIRCASES					-	-	
C2010	Stair Construction				-	-		
C2020	Stair Finishes				-	-		
C30	INTERIOR FINISHES					-	-	
C3010	Wall Finishes				-	-		
C3020	Floor Finishes				-	-		
C3030	Ceiling Finishes				-	-		
D10	CONVEYING SYSTEMS					-	-	
D1010	Elevators				-	-		
D1020	Escalators & Moving Walks				-	-		
D1030	Material Handling Systems				-	-		
D20	PLUMBING					-	-	
D2010	Plumbing Fixtures				-	-		
D2020	Domestic Water Distribution				-	-		
D2030	Sanitary Waste				-	-		
D2040	Rain Water Drainage				-	-		
D2050	Special Plumbing Systems				-	-		
D30	HVAC					-	-	
D3010	Energy Supply				-	-		
D3020	Heat Generating System				-	-		
D3030	Cooling Generating Systems				-	-		
D3040	Distribution Systems				-	-		
D3050	Terminal & Package Units				-	-		
D3060	Controls & Instrumentation				-	-		
D3070	Special HVAC Systems & Equipments				-	-		
D3080	Systems Testing & Balancing				-	-		
D40	FIRE PROTECTION					-	-	
D4010	Fire Protection & Sprinkler Systems				-	-		
D4020	Stand-pipe and Hose Systems				-	-		
D4030	Fire Protection Specialities				-	-		
D4040	Special Fire Protection Systems				-	-		
D50	ELECTRICAL					-	-	
D5010	Electrical Service & Distribution				-	-		
D5020	Lighting & Branch Wiring				-	-		
D5030	Communication and Security Systems				-	-		
D5040	Special Electrical Systems				-	-		
E10	EQUIPMENT					-	-	
E1010	Commercial Equipment				-	-		
E1020	Institutional Equipment				-	-		
E1030	Vehicular Equipment				-	-		
E1040	Other Equipment				-	-		
E20	FURNISHINGS					-	-	
E2010	Fixed Furnishings				-	-		
E2020	Movable Furnishings				-	-		
F10	SPECIAL CONSTRUCTION					-	-	
F1010	Special Structures				-	-		
F1020	Integrated Construction				-	-		
F1030	Special Construction Systems				-	-		

LEVELS OF AGGREGATION

ABBREVIATIONS

Figure III-5   Elemental Cost Model

Information

> *If I was given one hour to solve a problem on which*
> *my life depended, I would take 40 minutes to study it,*
> *15 minutes to review it and 5 minutes to solve it.*

Albert Einstein

The information phase consists of getting everybody on the value management team to understand the basic project/product information in the

FUNCTION Verb + Noun		COST		WORTH	
		$	%	$	%
		$0.00	0%	$0.00	0%
1	Verb + Noun	$0.00	0.00%	$0.00	
2	Verb + Noun	$0.00	0.00%	$0.00	
3	Verb + Noun	$0.00	0.00%	$0.00	
4	Verb + Noun	$0.00	0.00%	$0.00	
5	Verb + Noun	$0.00	0.00%	$0.00	
6	Verb + Noun	$0.00	0.00%	$0.00	
7	Verb + Noun	$0.00	0.00%	$0.00	
8	Verb + Noun	$0.00	0.00%	$0.00	
9	Verb + Noun	$0.00	0.00%	$0.00	
10	Verb + Noun	$0.00	0.00%	$0.00	
...	Verb + Noun	$0.00	0.00%	$0.00	

Figure III-6   Cost Worth Table

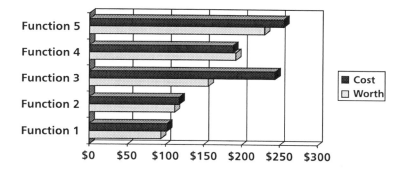

Figure III-7   Cost/Worth Model

same manner. A presentation of the objectives is made by the client, strategic issues usually are covered by the program manager, and tactical issues are presented by the project manager and/or the designers.

Stakeholders will attend both the information and the recommendation phases. During the information phase, they will confirm and validate data and commit to objectives; during the recommendation phase, they will accept recommendations and commit to implementation.

During the information phase, the scope of the study needs to be identified; a series of issues will be addressed in the presence of the stakeholders. They include but are not limited to: value study expected results, potential areas of impact, quality expectations (see Quality Modeling in Chapter IV), risk assessment (see Risk Analysis in Chapter IV), and partnering. Basically, partnering involves the recognition that there are many stakeholders on any given project. Each stakeholder has a role and also a specific vision of the project's success. **The objective of partnering is to have each stakeholder share his vision to realize visions are not mutually exclusive and that common goals can be shared**. The intention is to come to a mutual acceptance of different points of view for the sake of the project's success.

The principles stated in the section on Preparation in this chapter are not exclusive to the preparation/information phase but should be used throughout the workshop to confirm and/or assess changes in customer/client objectives and then to gather, validate, consolidate, model, and communicate incoming data to the team and stakeholders.

Presentation

The goal of the presentation is for the client and his team to clarify objectives and present the project and its issues. The team's goal is to comprehend these issues and resolve any unclear matter. The presentation will include strategic issues, which involve scope of project/study, quality expectations, deadlines, and budget; design (if at the design stage), involving rationale for the design, design criteria, systems and sub-systems, and alternative solutions (if any); tactical issues, including organizational structure, procurement, technical components, and production processes; and constraints, which involve codes and regulations, the environment, legal issues, and political issues.

The team leader will ensure that all team participants have the same understanding of the issues at stake. He will ask questions, restate, reiterate, and recapitulate until all team members and stakeholders agree on all the issues.

Function Analysis

If you accept the premise that understanding the problem is fifty percent of its solution, then separating the problem from its symptoms and effects by analyzing its functions is essential to the process.

J. J. Kaufman
American Value Specialist

In Search of the Need

Function analysis is what distinguishes value management from all other similar techniques and has enabled it to survive for fifty years as a recognized optimization and improvement method. It is the factor that enabled value management to be used in conjunction with or integrated into numerous fields and domains.

Function analysis abstracts technical solutions in order to concentrate on the actual needs and wants of the customer. It guides every participant (expert and lay-person) and stakeholder to a consensus on the objectives of a project because of its basic rhetoric. It is the foundation of change management because it enables abstraction of change requests to a level of basic needs that is much more stable and customer-oriented.

Item-oriented analysis involves looking at item A and asking, "How can item A be improved?" The result is item A', a modified version of item A; for example, trying to improve a bicycle may lead to a motorcycle.

Figure III-8   Item-Oriented Analysis

Value management involves looking at item A and asking, "How can the basic functions of item A be provided with a better value?" The result is item B, which sometimes is a completely different item. For example, if one of the basic functions of a bicycle is identified as "roll faster," the result will still be a motorcycle, but if the function is "move faster," item B could be an airplane.

Figure III-9   Function-Oriented Analysis

The discipline of function analysis requires that a function be described by using a verb and noun; adding an adjective often is helpful in identifying the problem being addressed and communicating the information outside the team. Certain verbs should be avoided—such as "provide" or "meet"—because they do not expand or contribute to the understanding of the function under study. It also is important to use active verbs, rather than passive; sometimes this is accomplished by using the noun as a verb and looking for a more pointed noun to describe the functions.

Passive:	Active:
Provide support	Support weight
Seek approval	Approve procedures
Develop exhibit	Exhibit products
Submit budget	Budget expenses
Determine resolution	Resolve problem

In integrated value management, the goal of function analysis is to identify, compare, and classify the functions in order to build a virtual, function-oriented model of the project (variation of the function analysis systems technique or FAST diagram) that the author calls function breakdown structure (FBS) in reference to project management's work breakdown structure (WBS). This model will, in turn, be used as a cost model with both cost and worth information in the pertinent blocks on the FAST diagram. This objective information helps identify the 20 percent of the functions which account for approximately 80 percent of the costs (Pareto's Law) and helps spot the functions with value mismatches (high cost/worth ratios).

A function analysis systems technique (FAST) diagram is versatile. In addition to its original uses for improving the function analysis and creativity phases of value engineering, it also can be used as a general purpose problem-solving tool with a wide range of complex problems. FAST also helps to improve communication and motivation, is objective, and provides a balanced approach between high-level function concepts and the task to be performed in order to implement those concepts.

Originally, the function analysis systems technique (FAST) was used to obtain cost reduction by simplifying and improving identification of the basic functions. FAST applications now have expanded to cover a diverse range of complex problems such as building construction, design-to-cost (DTC), motivation and incentive programs, medical diagnosis, systems analysis, procedure writing, management planning, and communications improvement. As time passes, even more applications appear likely for FAST diagrams.

The Function Analysis Workshop

It is essential that the participants in the workshop include representatives of the client involved with the project concept, development, execution, and use (see Figure II-4); needs and objectives should be defined and evaluated from every possible angle for the functional breakdown structure to be endorsed by every participant.

The job plan used by the author to conduct the function analysis workshop is based on a methodology developed in France and well described in Robert Tassinari's book *Le rapport qualité/prix* (Tassinari 1985, 61, 65–79). The method is divided into five steps, as follows:

1. IDENTIFY FUNCTIONS
—List functions (creative thinking)
—Define interaction and adaptation functions (environment analysis)
2. ORGANIZE FUNCTIONS (TASSINARI (1985) AND BRUN (1993) INVERT STEPS 2 AND 3; THE AUTHOR PREFERS BRUN'S VERSION, AS SHOWN HERE)
—Function Breakdown Structure *(Arbre fonctionnel)*
3. CHARACTERIZE FUNCTIONS (CAN BE COMBINED WITH QUALITY MODELING (KIRK 1994))
—Define measurement units and expected quality (criteria)
—Define flexibility level

4. Rank functions (In smaller or less complex projects, steps 4 and 5 and cost-worth model are often skipped.)

—Classify by order of relative importance

5. Rate functions

—Relative value weight (function cost distribution)

In the French method, the process is followed by the issuing of a document called the *Cahier des Charges Fonctionnel or CdCF* (function-based specifications).

In the case of project integration, the output of the workshop is a list of qualified functions, a function model, a quality model, and a cost-worth model that provide the basis of project planning, area definition, and space modeling in construction projects. These will, in turn, be used for budgeting purposes and to build the project work breakdown structure, all of which will be combined in the project plan.

During the function analysis workshop, the team can address issues of organizational structure and procurement and validate or establish a target cost and milestone schedule.

Identify Functions (Customer-Oriented)

For a well trained mind, a product is not an assembly of elements, but an assembly of functions.

Robert Tassinari

The first step in any project is to identify what it must do; in order to answer that question the team will identify the functions it must perform.

FUNCTION ANALYSIS TECHNIQUES

Creativity techniques should be combined with function identification techniques in order to ensure full coverage of the problem and team consensus.

Traditionally value analysis and value engineering have relied on the team's experience to identify functions in an intuitive way, a perfect solution as long as the sought functions were technically oriented. With the evolution of value management to provide a more customer-oriented focus, the use of this technique alone is no longer satisfying since "experience has proven that it will enable the team to identify only about 50% of the functions" (Tassinari 1985).

Many techniques have been developed over the years to specifically identify the functions of a project. Bytheway also used his function analysis systems technique (FAST) diagrams to promote and reinforce the creative process of finding alternatives to performing functions (1992, 229–32). Howard Ellegant uses a "Customer Attitude Survey" to identify the project's customer-oriented functions; he relies on a three- to four-hour "Focus Group" to define their acceptance criteria and rank them (1995).

In France value practitioners have developed a step-by-step function identification process that ensures complete identification of functions as well as of customer focus.

INTUITIVE RESEARCH

This phase is destined to identify functions based on an individual or a team's collective experience and knowledge of the problem. This is the traditional value engineering method. Approximately half the functions will be identified through this method.

ENVIRONMENT ANALYSIS (INTERACTORS METHOD)

In this phase, all elements external to the product that interact with it are identified as its environment; these elements are called interactors. The next step is to determine functions created from adaptation of these interactors to the product and vice versa.

Functions that exist between the interactors because of the product also should be noted; they are the interaction functions. For example, the need to ground a metal construction is evident when analyzing the relationship of lightning to the ground through the product.

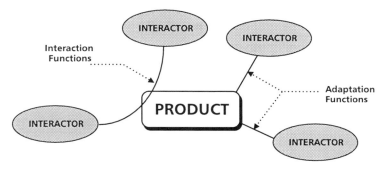

Figure III-10   Environment Analysis

This is probably the most important phase of the function identification process because it will establish the product in its setting, and the next phases will depend on it.

SEQUENTIAL ANALYSIS OF FUNCTIONAL ELEMENTS (SAFE)

This technique originated in the United States. Its objective is to identify all the different sequences of a product's life-cycle or use cycle; next, all functions derived from the performance of that product in its environment during its use sequence are identified.

ANALYSIS OF ACTIVITY AND STRESS

The logical extension to sequential analysis is to analyze the product's activities during use in order to identify both permanent and temporary stress to which it will be submitted. Functional requirements are then defined accordingly; for example, a product may have to withstand transportation over rough terrain and must therefore be able to resist severe shocks, or a building may have to withstand severe weather and should be built accordingly.

All of the above phases apply to a new product as well as to an existing product. **The following phases apply only if the product is already in the design phase or if it is an existing product.**

COMPARATIVE STUDY

This method consists of analyzing functions performed by one or more existing comparable products (including the competition's) and to identify essential, or unneeded, or merely interesting functions that had not occurred to the team. The product will be improved with the addition of new functions as long as great care is exercised in not assuming that technical functions are essential when they are not.

ANALYSIS OF CODES AND REGULATIONS

Products must incorporate functions required to meet applicable codes and regulations. These may vary from one domain and/or area to another, and their early identification ensures that the cost to meet these codes and regulations will be considered and optimized. The industry or the client's technical benchmarks should be considered on the same level.

MODEL ANALYSIS

Once the project is far enough into the design phase to identify its components or elements, they can be listed, and the identified functions can be assigned to each component or element. At that point, a model of the product is built and will be used by the team to reexamine each component or element in respect with the function(s) upon which it depends. This procedure is especially useful in the design phase of a project to eliminate costly components or elements that do not respond to an identified function and might have been added during design without reference to the previous function analysis.

Organize Functions (FAST Diagrams)

> *I'm forced, therefore, to state that FAST diagramming is an **art** rather than a **science**—but when properly applied, it's an art that reveals, as nothing else can, ways to improve value because through logic it stimulates our imagination and creativity.*

James E. Ferguson Jr.
American Value Specialist

After having identified functions, the value management team will undertake the task of organizing them into a coherent model. The organization of functions enables the team to verify the completeness of its identification process; it relies on two steps.

The first step is function expansion. For each function identified, three questions are asked: Why do you **verb noun**? How do you **verb noun**? When do you **verb noun**? Each question will be answered by another **verb noun** or one of the functions already identified. The question, "why," generates a higher-level function, and the question, "how," a lower-level function. Additional functions usually are identified, and this process helps in the preparation of function analysis systems technique (FAST) diagrams.

The second function is the function analysis system technique (FAST), which presents a graphical, structured representation of function relationship in response to the "why," "how," and "when" questions. It is effective in identifying functions that are not always evident, and it facilitates "directed" brainstorming sessions for better results.

CHARACTERISTICS OF FAST DIAGRAMS

"There is no 'correct' FAST model to compare with a text solution, but there is a 'valid' FAST model. Its degree of validity is directly dependent on the talents of the participating team members, and the scope of the related disciplines they can bring to bear on the problem. FAST is not complete until the model has the consensus of the participating team members and reflects their inputs" (Kaufman 1982).

The function analysis systems technique (FAST) aids in viewing the problem objectively and in defining the scope of the problem by showing the specific relationships of all functions with respect to each other. It also helps identify the basic function(s) and increases the probability that all of the functions have been identified and listed. FAST provides a basis for simplifying the total list of functions: eliminating those that are unnecessary and combining others that are necessary.

FAST APPLICATIONS

PROBLEM SOLVING

What is the problem? Why is a solution necessary? How can the solution be accomplished? By asking these questions about the main problem and its related higher-order and lower-order problems, a good understanding of the overall problem and its solution may be obtained. The function analysis systems technique (FAST) automatically helps find the "real" problem(s); breaks a large complex problem into manageable, individual problems; and provides a balanced approach between the overall, high-level aspects of a problem and the how-to-do-it actions required for the solution to the problem.

CREATIVITY

The function analysis systems technique (FAST) uses its "how" questions to stimulate creative thinking and thereby generate alternatives. The "how" questions are future-oriented; i.e., "How can it be done?" "How can it be improved?"

COMMUNICATIONS

Function analysis systems technique (FAST) diagrams provide a good base for communication. They let people know what is expected of them, why it is important, and, within limits, how they should perform the task. FAST provides a way to communicate complex information quickly.

CONSTRUCTION OF A FAST DIAGRAM

To begin drawing the function analysis systems technique (FAST) diagram, examine one particular function and ask "why" and "how" questions about that function. Each answer should include a verb and a noun, as in function analysis; the verb should be an action verb, and the noun should be measurable.

The "why" answer should be placed in a block to the left of the function, and the "how" answer should be placed in a block to the right of the function. Horizontally arranged functions—positioned as described earlier for the answers to the "why" and "how" questions—also must meet a time sequence requirement; i.e., the earlier time functions appear in relative time sequence starting at the right side of the FAST diagram.

Figure III-11   Basic FAST Diagram Construction

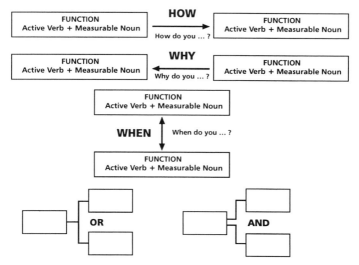

Figure III-12   FAST Key Words and Their Meanings

49

Functions that do not have a time-sequence relationship should be shown below or, in some cases, above a particular function in a horizontal line of functions. If the function happens at the same time and explains or elaborates another function, it should be placed below the horizontal path function. If the function occurs all the time, it should be placed above the horizontal path function at the extreme right of the diagram.

If there are specific design objectives, they should be placed above the basic function and shown as dotted boxes.

The scope of the study is shown with two dotted lines on the right and left. Higher-order function, or desired output, will lie to the immediate left scope line. The basic function always will lie to the immediate right of the left scope line. Any function supplying input to the problem, but not really part of it, should be outside the right scope line.

FAST COMPONENTS

Scope of the problem under study: Depicted as two vertical dotted lines, the scope lines bind the problem under study.

Highest order function(s): The objective or output of the basic function(s) and subject under study is described as highest-order function(s) and appears outside the left scope line to the left of the basic functions.

Lowest order function(s): Functions to the right, outside of the right scope line, represent the input side.

Basic function(s): Those function(s) to the immediate right of the left scope line representing the purpose or mission of the subject under study.

Concept: All functions to the right of the basic function(s) describe the approach elected to achieve the basic function(s).

Objectives or specifications: Objectives or specifications are particular characteristics or restrictions that must be achieved to satisfy the highest-order function; they are not in themselves functions. (**Note**: The use of objectives or specifications in the function analysis systems technique process is optional.)

Critical path functions: Any function on the "how" or "why" logic path is a critical path function.

Supporting functions: Supporting functions exist to achieve the performance levels specified in the objectives or because a particular approach was chosen to implement the basic function(s).

Dependent functions: Starting with the first function to the right of the basic function, each successive function is "dependent" on the one to its immediate left.

Independent (or supporting) function(s): Functions that do not depend on another function are located above the critical path function(s).

Activity: The method to perform a function (or group of functions).

TYPES OF FAST DIAGRAMS

Since Bytheway introduced his function analysis systems technique (FAST) diagramming method in 1965, many practitioners have devised their own versions of FAST. Ten years later, two of them had been used the most extensively and successfully by practitioners: the technically oriented (technical) FAST and the customer-oriented (task) FAST. In 1975, a five-day seminar/workshop was held at the University of Wisconsin-Madison, and its focus was on combining these versions. Participants included C. Bytheway, T. Snodgrass, T. C. Fowler, and W. Ruggles, among others. To the surprise of the organizers, the members of the committee agreed unanimously that each form of FAST has a definite application. Both are presented here, along with the conclusions of the committee.

Basically, one can state that the technical function analysis systems technique (FAST) applies best to existing products when one begins with an input, whereas task FAST and function breakdown structure (FBS) should be used for designing new products, starting with a task or need.

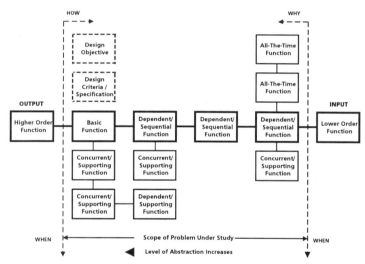

Figure III-13   Technically Oriented (Technical) FAST

The technical function analysis systems technique (FAST) works best on components that are part of a total product or design because the scope lines restrict the team or individual to the specific component. It also works better on an existing product analysis because you don't have to start with the higher-order function or task (the user or customer need).

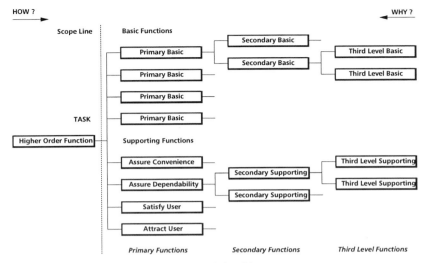

Figure III-14   Customer-Oriented (Task) FAST

The advantage of the task function analysis systems technique (FAST) is its ability to describe complete products or designs with one diagram. It also is more suited for new products to be designed because it insists on the customer concerns and always starts with a task (user or customer basic need).

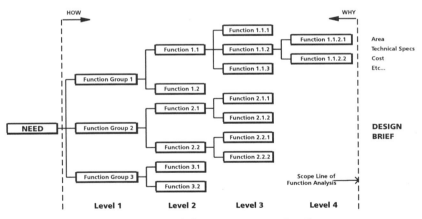

Figure III-15   Function Breakdown Structure (FBS)

The function breakdown structure evolved from the task function analysis systems technique (FAST) and mostly is destined for new products that will be developed from a need into measurable or assignable functions that will be used for design. It does not necessarily include the customer concerns or functions of the task FAST but is based on customer function identification. It is built very much in the same way as a work breakdown structure, in the sense that all the components of the project are contained at every level, and you build a function breakdown structure only to the level of detail needed to measure the function. Functions on a same level should be totally independent from each other and can even be contradictory.

If the environment analysis has been used to identify functions, function groups usually will correspond to interactors.

Characterize Functions

Ultimately, the functions are measured to create a project worth (NOT/MORE) that corresponds to the maximum overall resources expended to fulfill the customer's needs, objectives, and targets. The concept of function characterization involves the establishment of units of measure (criteria), by which the functions will be evaluated, the expected level of performance (worth) of each function, and the upper and lower limits of acceptance (flexibility). All this data will establish the benchmark according to which the function will be measured.

For example:

Function	Support Weight	Maintain Temperature
Criteria	Mass	Temperature
Level	80 Kg	20 °C
Tolerance	± 10 Kg	± 2 °C

CRITERIA

Criteria are used to define the type and unit of measurement by which the customer will judge or appreciate the performance of the product. Standard criteria are mass, temperature, speed, volume, consumption, distance, or radius, but other less measurable criteria also can be used, such as maintenance, durability, versatility, aesthetics, or color. When dealing with customer-oriented functions, one must be more sensible and be able to use more subjective units of measure.

LEVEL

The level is the measure of the expected performance against which alternatives will be judged or assessed later in the study. This reference can be established according to codes and regulations or to industry standards or, again, to less substantial concepts established by the client. It will be the value practitioner's job to find ways to evaluate what the client might mean by comfort or pleasant or not too loud, and so on.

TOLERANCE

Once the criteria and level are secure, a tolerance range must be established in order to fix the lower and upper acceptable limits. Again, the customer will be the judge, and the value practitioner must be his guide.

It is important to note that some characteristics may have a zero-tolerance range for performance acceptability. The characteristic either is met successfully, or the product is not acceptable, e.g., the "John Deere" tractor's yellow and green color.

Rank Functions

The methods of ranking functions are very similar to those used to rank ideas in the creativity phase. C. Fallon, D.H. Stafford, and others have devised very sophisticated methods for ranking ideas and functions. The French methodology promotes a simple subjective method of ranking with a one to five coefficient: (1) useful, (2) necessary, (3) important, (4) very important, and (5) essential.

Many other value practitioners, like S. Kirk and H. Ellegant, for example, also promote the use of a simple method like this one for ranking functions (Smith, Hinchman & Grylls 1993; Ellegant 1995); it is amazingly efficient, and more sophisticated methods are not necessarily worth the effort.

Rate Functions

Rating the functions is the third step leading to the creativity phase after identifying and organizing/characterizing/ranking the functions. Using cost as an example, the cost of each function must be estimated in order to direct the creativity phase toward the functions that have the most optimization potential.

When the study is directed toward optimizing an existing product, this task is very easy to accomplish. The product's components are put on one side of a matrix and the functions on the other side; the total cost of the product is then distributed among its components, and the cost of each component is distributed among the functions it fulfills. The goal is not to assign the exact cost to each function but rather to get a good idea in terms of percentage of the function's worth.

As more new fields of practice are opening to value management, it is important that value practitioners do not limit their ratings of functions to cost as the only measuring unit that can be assigned to a product or project through this method. Quality, time, human resources, risks, communication, and whatever other data will be determined by the customer's needs also should be used. A good example of this is quality modeling developed by S. Kirk of Smith, Hinchman & Grylls (SH&G) (Kirk 1994).

FUNCTION WORTH

In review, worth is the minimum acceptable ratio of performance against expenditure of resources. When an actual product is being studied, the goal is to allocate resources for each function according to the proportion of the global cost needed to fulfill this particular function. When the product being studied does not exist, or when it is not satisfactory, it becomes essential to assign each function the minimum expected expenditure of resources needed to fulfill it. This is a subjective procedure whereby the exchange value is judged by the team.

A reference model (worth model) can then be created for future comparison of alternatives. The cost of alternatives will be compared to this worth model in order to calculate the **value index** and identify cost/worth mismatches. Value index is the monetary relationship (ratio) of function worth to function cost, where the highest value is one.

The value study's objective is to seek the course that will generate the greatest benefits for the least cost. Most benefits can be expressed in terms of money but many cannot. Non-monetary benefits include aesthetics or image, expansion potential, functional relationships, flexibility or versatility, safety or reliability, reduction of environmental impact, political considerations, and sales and marketing. It is important to consider those non-monetary benefits during the study, particularly when allocating measurement units to functions.

Creativity

> *All Human Development, no matter what form it takes, must be outside the rules; otherwise, we would never have anything new.*
>
> Charles Franklin Kettering
> English Inventor

In Search of the Solution

The creativity phase consists of producing the greatest possible number of ideas in a short period of time. It is very important to remember that the value management process involves alternative use of the left and right sides of the brain. During the creativity phase, there is no room for judgment; **think creatively, then evaluate critically.**

Creativity groups provide:
- Good mix of people with no major power relationships.
- Positive attitude; belief that the project can be improved.
- Good communication; remove mental blocks.
- Free-flowing ideas; no logical sequence.
- And remember that all great ideas seem absurd when first proposed.
  Creative individuals possess:
- Motivation; persistence of drive.
- Flexibility in thinking; ability to abstract.
- Sensitivity to the problem.

- Originality; openness to change.
- Tolerance to ambiguity.
  The Creativity process addresses the following items:
- The problem itself.
- Interacting problems.
- Risk factors: conflicts, resources, constraints, and so on.
- Additional undiscovered benefits.
- Implementation.

Creativity Applications in Value Management

Creative thinking is a product of the imagination where a new combination of thoughts and things are brought together.

Lawrence D. Miles

It is important in value management to direct the creative process. Again, Pareto's Law has demonstrated that 20 percent of the functions or elements of a problem hold 80 percent of the resources expenditure. Therefore, it is a loss of time and energy to concentrate on the 80 percent that hold only 20 percent of the optimization potential.

In an iterative value process like integrated value management, it is important to reevaluate the "costly" functions or elements before each workshop because the preceding action will have changed the cost distribution.

Certain guidelines can be given as to which items should be prioritized in a value management creativity session: items with high immediate or life-cycle resource expenditure; continuous or repetitive resource expenditure; high-risk items with undefined criteria; code or regulation-associated items or constraints that appear unreasonable; and items with high cost/worth ratio and above average user complaints.

The team leader should ensure that the environment stays creative, enabling ideas to thrive during the entire creativity phase. For that matter, he should encourage "creativity synergists" and discourage "creativity inhibitors"; he also must beware of "road-blocks" or "idea killers."

Creativity Synergists

Some circumstances—such as discontentment with the status quo and curiosity, motivation, and perseverance—create a favorable setting for creativity. Others include competition and necessity; no constraints or "sacred cows"; ignorance of the past; originality, open-mindedness, and flexibility; liberty to advance ideas without criticism; effective interdisciplinary communications; good human relations, respect, and recognition; working with peers; and strong management support and participation.

Creativity Inhibitors

Other factors create a negative environment for creativity; they include rigid and unbending rules, unwritten guidelines, fear to fail or of ridicule, contentment with status quo, negative comments or roadblocks, judgment, bureaucratic processes involving red tape, and intimidating superiors or colleagues.

Roadblocks

Roadblocks are statements that cut ideas short; they stifle idea association and endanger the creativity process. They usually are exploited by people who exercise influence. Value management practitioners should be aware of them and keep them out of the workshop.

Here are 25 good "idea killers":

1. It's not realistic!
2. Why change it?
3. It's been working for 25 years!
4. This is not the right time.
5. It's not part of our mandate.
6. It would be too difficult to manage.
7. Let's form a committee!!!
8. It would modify habits too much.
9. It's a STUPID idea!
10. It will never work...
11. It's a good idea, BUT ...
12. It does not apply to us.
13. We have already thought about it!?!
14. Let's wait a little more...
15. It'll cost too much.
16. Management will never agree.
17. We've already tried it.
18. It doesn't correspond to standards!
19. We're already too far ...
20. We'd have to start all over again.
21. We don't have time.
22. Think about security?
23. It's technically impossible.
24. No!
25. No! No!! **NO!!!**

Form

LISTING IDEAS

CREATIVITY PHASE   **LIST OF IDEAS**

Function: ...   Page: 00

Element: ...   Sub-element: ...

No.	Alternative	A/R *	Comments
1.			
2.			
3.			
4.			
5.			
6.			
7.			
8.			
9.			
10.			
11			
12.			
13.			
14.			
15.			
16.			
17.			
18.			
19.			
20.			
21.			
22.			
23.			
24.			
25.			

"LIST IDEAS WITHOUT JUDGMENT"   * A: Accepted R: Rejected

Evaluation

Seek the Best, not Perfection.

Stephen J. Kirk
American Value Specialist

Don H. Stafford very thoroughly described the different evaluation options offered to the value study team in his article, "The Judgment Phase—More Than One Way to Skin a Cat," which is the main source for this section (1995).

The purpose of the evaluation phase is to identify and select the best ideas for further development. It is a fact that the team does not have enough time to develop all of the good ideas; therefore, the workshop process must focus on the best ideas for development in order to achieve the best value. Efficiency in adequately developing those ideas that have the most merit is as important as their development.

The team and leader must determine a methodology to identify the best ideas in a time-efficient fashion. Experience indicates that there are three criteria that appear again and again in idea evaluation: inherent value of the ideas; expected cost savings; and likelihood of the owner and designer acceptance.

The process used to accomplish the judgment phase must set limits on the number of ideas to be developed. The team should first segregate ideas, identify priorities, and then separate those ideas to be developed from those to be discarded.

Segregation of ideas involves dividing the ideas into different categories. In general, four groups of ideas are identified: ideas that diminish resource expenditure; ideas that avoid resource expenditure; ideas that improve project performance; and ideas that increase resource expenditure but still result in better value.

Priority identification focuses the team's effort on ideas that should be developed first. It also may separate ideas that the team will develop from those it will try to develop only if there is enough time. Most importantly, a line must be drawn to separate those ideas to be developed from those which will be discarded. This requires proper application of the combined judgment, knowledge, and experience of those drawing the line.

The first rule of evaluation is to eliminate all ideas that do not have obvious reasons to be kept for development. Once this rule is set, the team will establish the rules for selection and ranking of the ideas to be developed and then will choose a method of rating ideas.

Basically, there are three selection/ranking methods available to choose those ideas that will be kept for development; each has multiple choices: leader decision, majority decision, and consensus. **Rating criteria** can vary from a simple "accepted—rejected" to more sophisticated weighed matrix methods with lots of variables. Again, the time allocated to development and the type of study will decide which path should be chosen.

Eliminating Ideas

In order to be kept for development, each idea must have a "champion" who will defend that idea and lead its development. If an idea does not find a champion, it is eliminated. Unfeasibility of the idea within the scope (time, cost, and so on) of the project can be a good argument to reject it, except if it is an idea with so much value that it is worth changing the project parameters. If it is established that there is no chance for an idea to be accepted by the client/customer, there is no sense in pursuing it.

Selection/Ranking Methods

LEADER DECISION

The leader decision approach casts the value manager team leader in a dictator role based on his own judgment and experience, as input from other team members is not included in this type of judgment process.

There are, however, some advantages. First, it is very fast. With an inexperienced team, it circumvents a very time-consuming process, as the team members learn while performing the judgment. Also, if the owner or designer has specific focus issues, it ensures that they are considered. It maximizes the time for idea development.

Of course, there are disadvantages, as well. It does not provide for incorporation of the knowledge and experience of the entire team and can result in the team missing some good ideas. Also, it requires a very strong leader, particularly if the team members are experienced in value engineering.

LEADER DECISION WITH DISCUSSION

A variation of the leader decision technique adds a second step consisting of the discussion and review of the decisions. If a team member champions a "don't develop" or "design suggestion" idea, this idea is re-examined. The leader continues to have the last word, but additional information is gained from the team members. Another way is to ask each team member to review the ideas in his discipline area. Proposed changes are discussed briefly, but the final decision is still made by the leader.

An advantage of this method is that although it's not as fast as the leader decision process, it also is fast. Another advantage is that it includes the element of team member experience, allowing input from the technical expertise of the entire team, and increases the quality of the idea selection process. If the client has identified specific focus, it ensures consideration, and it still provides significant time for idea development. This method allows team members to spend time in a very efficient fashion, providing input to edit, rather than create, the initial judgments. The disadvantages are that this technique requires a strong leader and takes more time than both the leader decision and the voting process.

MAJORITY DECISION

The first step of the majority decision approach is the determination of how many votes are required for an idea to be developed. The second step consists of voting for those ideas deemed to have merit. Each team member is given an equal number of votes, normally half to three quarters of the total number of ideas which can be developed. The team should be instructed to vote following these guidelines: no more than one vote per person for an idea; vote for the ideas that are best for all disciplines; vote independently of the other team members; and vote in your discipline first. The cut-off is determined based on the number of ideas the team can develop.

This method is very fast; it combines speed with input from the entire team. It is particularly useful when conducting short-duration studies and when the issues are relatively straightforward. At the same time, its disadvantage is that it offers little opportunity for interaction between the team members.

VOTING WITH DISCUSSION

The voting with discussion methodology is a modification of the voting process; it adds a discussion step. If discussion is conducted before the vote, each idea is debated briefly with no more than two individuals permitted to make comments in favor or against the idea. If discussion occurs after the vote, it is limited to those ideas that someone feels have been wrongly judged. The after-voting discussion is more efficient in terms of time required.

Among this method's advantages is that it combines speed with input from the entire team and is particularly useful when conducting short duration studies. Its main disadvantage is that it provides only limited documentation of the selection process.

CONSENSUS

The consensus methodology is either a one-step or a two-step process: discuss and rate ideas; and/or check against production capacity and re-rate if needed. There are two important decisions to be made before using this method: which selection method to use for dispute resolution and which rating system to use. Regardless of which selection method or rating system is used, the technique encourages input from all team members. The total number of ideas selected for development still must be compared against the development capacity of the team.

This approach is particularly effective when the team focuses quickly on the salient issues in the discussion. It is most applicable in longer workshops and is very valuable when important owner priorities exist but are not easily defined. When owner representatives are present in the workshop, this is probably the most effective methodology for incorporating owner input into the judgment process.

This method's main disadvantage is that it takes a lot of time to properly accomplish consensus; judgment takes place in an environment of free discussion that can easily get out of hand.

Rating

SIMPLE RATING SYSTEM

There are basically three approaches to the simple rating system. The first is a system using a numerical rating from one to ten, with ten representing the best and one, the worst. Most value team leaders omit the number five in this system because it does not reflect a choice. Experience indicates that with this system it is difficult to prevent the team from wasting time debating small rating differences in the ideas. Yet, Jerry Kaufman has developed an effective one to ten rating system that he calls "GFI," or "Gut Feel Index" (1992). It involves the use of "flash cards" that go from "no way, too risky" (one) to "super, go—a winner" (ten).

The second system either uses numerical ratings or letters (A, B, C, and so on). This is a very effective system in the sense that it allows enough latitude for judgment while, at the same time, limits discussion. The rating usually is set as follows: 4 or A indicates that these ideas will be developed; 3 or B means that these ideas will be developed if the team has enough time; 2 or C suggests that although these ideas have some merit, they will not be developed by the value engineering team (optional); and 1 or D indicates that these ideas have little merit and, therefore, should not be considered.

The third system is a simple pass/fail system that usually is expressed by "accepted" (A) or "rejected" (R).

LIST OF ADVANTAGES/DISADVANTAGES
This method consists of establishing the advantages and disadvantages of each idea and then comparing them to each other. It is very effective when examining alternatives to an existing product or design, but it is less useful for a new product or project. It also is less objective when ranking functions.

WEIGHED MATRIX
The weighed matrix evaluation method is the most complex and time-consuming of all the methods discussed here. Good examples of weighed matrix are the **combinex** method developed by Fallon and the **weighed evaluation** and **quality modeling** methods developed by Steve Kirk and Smith, Hinchman & Grylls (SH&G), as well as the **evaluation** method described by H.R. Sandberg (Fallon 1965; Smith, Hinchman & Grylls 1993; Kirk 1994; Sandberg 1983).

The weighed matrix method requires at least four steps to accomplish (eight steps for combinex): (1) select evaluation criteria; (2) assign relative weights to criteria; (3) evaluate each alternative against the criteria; and (4) compare and select the alternatives offering best value. This method is the most sophisticated of all evaluation methods, and it can be used with many variations. Each practitioner is encouraged to explore this process to find the optimal variation for his own needs.

SELECT CRITERIA
It is best to limit the number to about five to fifteen criteria; the selection of the criteria is very important to the validity of this judgment method. Each criterion must be independent of the others and specific to the project

under review. Only criteria that have significant impact for the customer should be listed. As for functions, technical criteria should not constitute most of the selected criteria. Letters work much better than numbers for identifying criteria because there is no rating attached to letters.

ASSIGN CRITERIA WEIGHTS

If only two or three criteria are to be used, it will be relatively simple to attach an appropriate weighting of the criteria. When more criteria are being considered, the basic method accomplishes the weighting between only two criteria at a time. Comparisons are to be based on two assumptions: all alternatives meet at least minimum requirements for each criterion, and, when choosing between two criteria, the other remains constant. When comparing two criteria, many issues can be considered; Smith, Hinchman & Grylls (SH&G) suggests conducting the discussion along the lines of needs versus desires, important versus unimportant, and trade-off versus non trade-off.

If there is no significant difference, both are entered into the square; otherwise the letter of the dominating criterion is entered into the square. The evaluator determines the level of preference; the weighting number (1@3 to 1@5) is then entered into the square following the letter. The criterion with the highest score is assigned a weight of ten in the weight column, and the weights for the other criteria are calculated proportionally.

For optimal objectivity, the calculation of the weights should not be done until after the evaluation of alternatives has been completed. For greatest effectiveness the weighted evaluation process should be a "blind" process.

EVALUATE ALTERNATIVES

Evaluation of the alternatives is accomplished by measuring the performance of each idea or alternative against the criteria developed during the previous exercise. Ideas will be given a score of either five, representing excellent, four or very good, three or good, two or fair, and one or poor, considering how each idea ranks against each criterion. As each score may vary from individual to individual, it is important that the customer be represented during this phase or at least has the opportunity to review and comment on the scores.

In the case of trade-offs, it is important that alternatives meet the customer's minimal requirements; in other words, a balance should always exist between the expected quality and the resources needed to attain it.

SELECT CUT-OFF POINT

Before selecting alternatives, the team should quickly review the results of the evaluation for any obvious distortions and readjust the score accordingly. Sometimes distinctions are fairly obvious; sometimes they are not. The professional judgment of the leader and the team members—in combination with an assessment of the time available for development, to select those ideas to be developed further, and to determine the order in which they should be developed—must be relied upon.

The chief advantage of this method is that, when properly executed, it is the most thorough of all methods. It is most useful when there are a relatively small number of options to be evaluated, and the relative merits are either not clearly obvious or not developed to a sufficient degree to permit selection of the best alternatives by one of the faster methods.

It is a very valuable method when evaluating projects at the planning stage. It also is useful when a few of the options need deeper evaluation, even though a majority of the alternatives may be selected by another method. It is more appropriate in lengthy studies and provides the best documentation.

Yet, its disadvantage is that a great deal of time is required to evaluate each alternative. It is less useful on short studies and on studies in which a wide range of alternatives are desirable.

Delphi Method

The Delphi method was developed at the Rand Corporation in the fifties. It consists of experts evaluating ideas on an individual basis in a series of cycles until consensus is reached. The objective is to obtain a true consensus with the least possible compromise due to group influence.

This method can be useful for a product under development since the process is very similar to the iterative design process and enables identifying risk areas and potential optimization alternatives in a more timely manner than performing the entire design process. However, as for the weighted matrix, it should be used on a limited number of ideas and only when the problem under study is well defined; otherwise, it can be very time consuming.

Conclusions

Each of the judgment methods described possesses strong and weak points. The degree of applicability of each to an individual workshop varies with the study duration, skill level and personality of the team leader, and the complexity of project issues. For general use, the leader decision with discussion, majority decision, and voting with discussion methods probably are the most effective. The weighted matrix method is valuable for longer workshops in which very comprehensive recommendations should appear. Usually the 1@4 simple rating system combined with the voting with discussion method is a good compromise between efficiency and effectiveness.

It is recommended, though, that one bear in mind that all of these methods are valuable only if they relate to the customer's needs. Value depends on quality, schedule, and functionality as much as on capital cost and life-cycle cost.

Weighted Matrix Example

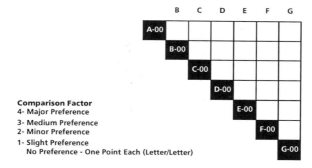

Comparison Factor
4- Major Preference
3- Medium Preference
2- Minor Preference
1- Slight Preference
No Preference - One Point Each (Letter/Letter)

CRITERIA WEIGHTING

Criteria		Raw Score	Weight (0-10)
A			
B			
C			
E			
F			
G			

EVALUATION MATRIX

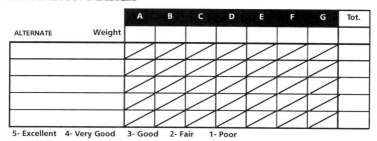

5- Excellent   4- Very Good   3- Good   2- Fair   1- Poor

Development

The development phase of a value study is the prelude to the recommendation phase. Both phases are linked by the same objective; i.e., convince the client's team that the proposed alternatives are worth implementing. The main reason for this phase is to prepare proposal implementation by developing the alternatives that have been identified in the previous phase.

Favoring Implementation

In order to favor implementation, it is very useful, at this stage, to review the customer-oriented values or objectives that have been

---

identified earlier. In the case of integrated value management, it is advisable to reconsider or revalidate those objectives, since they might have evolved during the course of the project. It also is advisable to brainstorm about who the decision-makers are and what their specific benefits will be.

Technical studies—as well as feasibility, quality, life-cycle costs, time, and risk impact assessment—will be conducted on each value management proposal (VMP). Value management proposals should be SMART, that is: specific, measurable, achievable, realistic, and time-framed.

It is important, in order to optimize the number of proposals that can be studied and presented to the client, to detail these studies to the minimum required to enable the stakeholders to make a sensible decision. More than one alternate can be suggested for each proposal in order to give a choice of options to the stakeholders in consideration of issues at hand. The value team must beware of presenting too many proposals or options, thereby diluting the significance of each of them.

Classifying and Estimating Proposals

Before any other step is undertaken, value management proposals are classified by trade, component, element, function, or any other explicit system compatible with the client's objectives. All similar value management proposals are grouped and/or combined. Only the distinctive ones are kept; all those that relate to the same concept are considered as alternates or eliminated. The goal is to bring the number of proposals to a minimum and eliminate repetition.

In order to choose the value management proposals that should be presented to the client, and considering that a thorough selection has already been done in the previous phase, the most important issue at this stage is their implementation potential.

DETAILED TECHNICAL DEVELOPMENT

Each proposal will be supported by a detailed technical analysis. The value management proposal will be compared to the actual situation or expected performance objective; if the objective cannot be reached, reasons will be provided.

COSTING

At this stage, all cost assumptions will be validated and documented by the team's cost experts. Life-cycle costs will be calculated for each value management proposal and used to compare each alternate. Savings or increases in costs will be identified.

IDENTIFICATION OF CONSTRAINTS

Constraints and conditions of implementation are addressed for each value management proposal and alternate. The range of constraints and conditions should be the same for all proposals. Comparisons must be made on the same assumptions that are to be documented; compare "apples to apples," so to speak.

All constraints pertaining to the value management proposal (codes, environment, legal issues, and so on), as well as conditions of implementation (redesign, delays, increase in capital cost, change in cash flow, quality, and so forth) should be documented and assessed; mitigation methods will be determined.

FEASIBILITY STUDY

For each proposal, the value study will determine the expected pay-back period; i.e., cost of value management proposal versus time to reach break-even point. The team will perform a benefit/risk analysis by assessing the expected risks versus the expected benefits. These can be monetary or non-monetary, but the measurement unit must be the same for both the risk and the benefit.

Value Management Proposals (VMP) Forms

DETAILED VALUE MANAGEMENT PROPOSAL FORM

DEVELOPMENT PHASE   **VALUE MANAGEMENT PROPOSALS**

Function: **VMP NO:**

                                                                        Page: 01

Element: Sub-element:

Current Design Cost: $

Description of current design, Criteria, Alternates, Benefits, Risks, Analysis and Recommendation

_____

_____

_____

_____

_____

_____

_____

_____

Note: If needed, add sketches, calculations, estimates, and other pertaining documents

Summary of Present Value (PV) of potential savings and classification of alternates

ALTERNATE	1	2	3	4
CAPITAL COST	$	$	$	$
ENERGY COST	$	$	$	$
O&M COST	$	$	$	$
TOTAL PV	$	$	$	$
CLASSIFICATION				

LIST OF VALUE MANAGEMENT PROPOSALS
Development Phase

LIST OF VALUE MANAGEMENT PROPOSALS

Element or
Disciplne:

Page:

VMP No.	Description	Cost of current design	Reduction (Increase)		Class.	Status
			Capital	O & M		
1.						
2.						
3.						
4.						
5.						
6.						
7.						
8.						
9.						
10.						
11						
12.						
13.						
14.						
15.						
16.						
17.						
18.						
19.						
20.						

* When VMPs constitute alternates of the same proposal, only one cost should be included in the total cost of reductions.

** Status: A (Accepted) R (Rejected) P (Pending)

SUMMARY OF VALUE MANAGEMENT PROPOSALS

MERIT / DELAY	A	B	C	TOTAL
1	$	$	$	$
2	$	$	$	$
3	$	$	$	$
TOTAL	$	$	$	$

1. TECHNICAL MERIT

A. No reduction of Quality or Performance
B. Acceptable reduction of Quality or Performance
C. Major reduction of Quality or Performance

2. IMPLEMENTATION DELAY

1. One week or less
2. From 1 to 6 weeks
3. More than 6 weeks

3. Total estimated implementation cost $

4. Total of potential savings $

5. Percentage of potential savings %

6. Capital cost increase (if any) $

7. Present value of future savings (LCC) (years) $

Note: Redesign costs are not included unless otherwise specified.

Recommendation

Customers buy benefits, not features. [...] Buying is a highly subjective, personalized process of determining relative value.

Gregory D. Githens
Project Manager

The presentation/recommendation phase's objective is to demonstrate the overall value increase potential for the project, as well as that of each individual proposal. The value team's recommendations and proposal implementation conditions are presented to the stakeholders for their approval and final decision on implementation.

Recommendations You Can't Refuse

It is advisable to decide the format of recommendations before developing the proposals in order to be able to focus on the elements that are relevant to the chosen type of presentation.

IDENTIFYING THE TARGET(S) (WHO)

The team should identify key managers to attend the presentation of proposals. They must have the power to make decisions and will form the steering committee. The "champion" of implementation usually is the project manager; the team must envision the ways in which the implementation of proposals will benefit both the executive and the manager.

REVIEWING THE OBJECTIVES (WHY)

In view of the results of the study, the value team will review the objectives that have been identified at the beginning of the workshop and reexamined regularly during the study. They will assess their continued relevance and modify the perspective of the value proposals, if necessary. These objectives will be presented as a way of introduction in order to remind everyone of the issues at stake.

PRESENTING THE CONCLUSIONS (WHAT)

The presentation of conclusions should be specific, measurable, achievable, realistic, and time-framed as well as "short and sweet." Recommendations should be direct and contain a summary of the expected benefits for each specific stakeholder.

The following are to be included in the presentation of each proposal: selection criteria, life-cycle cost analysis, non-monetary issues, and implementation conditions (redesign, additional studies, procurement impact, validation, delays, and so on).

RECOMMENDING SOLUTIONS

During the information phase, the team listed potential areas of impact for the study. They assessed risks associated with the implementation of those results, confirmed quality expectations, and explored partnering issues. If this procedure has been iterated throughout the study—by integrating project management and value management—surprises will be greatly reduced during the implementation process. Also, ways of dealing with unexpected occurrences will be provided, thereby easing value management proposal implementation.

Each value team member will be given the task of persuading management of her respective group to endorse the value proposals. J. J. Kaufman suggests the formation of a management "steering committee" that will accomplish the following steps: management deliberation, decision (go/no go), establish priority, assign responsibilities, allocate resources, and follow up (1992).

It is advisable to get the expected members of this "committee" to attend the presentation in order to obtain commitments on the spot. For that reason, an implementation plan must be prepared and an implementation "champion" has to be identified during the presentation.

THE IMPLEMENTATION PLAN

The first step of the implementation plan is to identify the individuals responsible for implementation; usually, it is the project manager's role. The team will try to secure that individual's commitment to implement the value management proposals as well as a commitment from management to support him.

The implementation plan will provide for effectively planned tasks and activities throughout the project management process; approval and control points should be established through a sensible milestone schedule. An implementation success measurement method and report process is to be included in the plan, as well. Targeted value procedures can be planned in case of deviation from the plan.

Types of Presentation

REPORTS

Written reports are the evidence that remains after the flare is gone. They should be well organized and cover the value study process in detail. There are basically two types of reports: management report and detailed report. A typical table of contents is presented here for both types of reports.

Management Report
A. Executive Summary
B. Background of Project (goals, expectations, parameters, constraints, and so on)
C. Objectives of the Value Study
1. Reestablish Goals
2. Restate the Problem
D. Summary of Proposals
E. Benefits
F. Recommendations
G. Implementation Plan (including implementation conditions)
H. Conclusions

Detailed Report
A. Introduction
1. List of participants
2. Agenda
3. Job Plan
4. Outline of Value Study Process
B. Classification of Value Management Proposals (VMP)
C. Summary of Value Management Proposals
D. Detailed Value Management Proposals grouped by function/element/component
1. List of proposals
2. Detailed proposal
E. Annexes
1. Complete list of ideas from creativity phase
2. Backup for estimates, life-cycle costs, quality, risk assessment, and other supporting evidence
3. Supporting material (plans, technical specs, standards, regulations, and so on)

AUDIO-VISUAL

It is always advisable to use visual aids to enhance the presentation of proposals. High-quality overheads are quite easy to prepare with today's computer programs and have a high impact. It also is facile to prepare a computerized presentation if one has a computer screen projector. Visual aids always should be considered as a tool to enhance communication and not as an end in themselves.

VERBAL

There always is a need for a verbal presentation to the client. Each "champion" usually will present his recommended proposals and discuss them.

Managers are always very busy; therefore, the total presentation should not last more than one-half hour to one hour. The presentation should be organized accordingly and priority given to the value management proposals with the most value and/or implementation potential.

Verbal presentation is organized into three steps: identify subject (objectives and conclusions); present in detail, listing pros and cons; and repeat and emphasize conclusions.

Follow Up of Implementation

> *In modern VA [value analysis], Implementation is step one. [...] Implementation rates of a properly conducted VA study are typically very near 100%.*
>
> Theodore C. Fowler
> American Value Specialist

First, it is important to understand that **it is not the value team or leader's role to implement value proposals**. Too often in the past, though, value practitioners have not focused on implementation; they have been satisfied with a "potential" percentage of savings. In today's competitive market, however, value practitioners must follow up on the value proposals of the value study. This is where the "ilities" of a project become handy again as a checklist. Typically, the following stakeholders have to be supported.

THE CUSTOMER

The customer might need to reassess a proposal against his needs. If his needs evolve during the project, the value practitioner will need to restate them. Every proposal should bear a benefit for the customer and consider its affordability.

THE PROJECT MANAGER

The value practitioner will assist the project manager in the evaluation of change proposals regarding producibility (constructibility), and, in project team meetings, to answer questions about the value management process and the proposals. Sound value management proposals should aid the project manager to avoid potential problems and risks.

THE DESIGNERS

The designers should be paid if value management proposals involve redesigning as part of the project; the value management practitioner should support them. He also will help with the development of proposals. Each proposal that affects the quality of the design (functional or technical) should be reviewed and approved by the designers.

The Operations and Management Manager

The value practitioner is supporting the operations and management people when assessing the reliability, maintainability, availability, and operability of each proposal.

The Marketing Team

The value team will ensure that the proposals will improve the product's marketing capabilities.

The Users

The users (consumers) care about usability, flexibility, and social acceptability, all which should be considered. The users' needs should be included in the customer's needs.

CHAPTER IV

Value Integration

Examining Project Management Methodologies

We must end the debate about whether the Value methodology is what should be used "instead of" something else, and recognize that it is a valuable tool to be used in concert with or in support of other programs.

Ginger Adams, President
Society of American Value Engineers, 1996

Many new management techniques come and go every year; a few have been around for a while and seem to be here to stay. Project management (PM), total quality management (TQM), design to cost (DTC), risk management, and partnering are among those techniques which can be combined or integrated with value management. Some other techniques have been developed and incorporated into value studies and have become methodologies in their own right. These include function analysis, quality modeling, cost/worth modeling, customer-oriented value engineering (COVE), strategic value planning (SVP), and *Cahier des charges fonctionnel* (CdCF). Value practitioners should be aware of the existence and the use of these methodologies and techniques in order to be able to integrate them, when required, or to use value management when exercising them.

We will now examine three of these methodologies and their integration into value management.

Risk Analysis

There's never enough time to do it right the first time, but there is always enough time to do it over if it's wrong.

R. Max Wideman,
Fellow, Project Management Institute

Risk analysis is becoming more and more unavoidable in project management. Project managers now are asked to identify and assess risks as well as to find solutions to mitigate them. Risk experts have developed their knowledge into an elaborated statistical science that is not easily accessible to the lay-person, namely: the client.

Risk management, though, is a rather simple proactive process that can be integrated easily into the value management study. Risk management integration can improve the impact of value proposal implementation by making the customer aware of potential risks and solutions to avoid or mitigate them. Thomas E. Papageorge of the Georgia Institute of Technology, has developed a simple way to integrate risk management into the concept and development stages of a project (1988); it is outlined here.

What Is Risk?

Risk is defined as an exposure to the possibility of loss or damage to people, property, or other interests. Risks are present in every aspect of doing business and offering services, ranging from the most obvious and simple problems to obscure and highly complex situations.

The first step in controlling risks is learning to perceive and categorize them. In order to perceive all possible risk situations, the risk manager must have a clear understanding of risk. For some businesses, risk is a potential problem that must be avoided at all costs. For others, risks are an accepted part of business that must be controlled and managed.

Unsolved risk problems often terminate in litigation. Typical risk losses or harm can include loss of reputation and/or business, reduction in qualified personnel, loss of revenue, physical harm to employees, physical damage to the project, reduction in the quality of the project, and bankruptcy.

RISK IDENTIFICATION

The risk manager cannot always anticipate every risk involved in a project. However, it is helpful to try and identify as many risks as possible, including improbable risks. There are a few principles to follow in order to increase risk identification. It is essential to identify all potential risks—all levels, from internal to external—as early as possible; do not allow any problem to go unnoticed or unresolved. Closely evaluate every participant's ability to perform, including both shortcomings and strengths. Evaluate contractual conditions and obligations, ensuring that contracts are comprehensive, precise, and fair. Evaluate existing project conditions, taking care to identify project restraints or constraints that might result in loss or harm, and, finally, provide and implement a systematic risk problem identification procedure.

PHASES OF RISK

Risk can easily go unnoticed until it has developed into loss or harm. The risk manager should be aware that every risk has three phases: potential problem, actual occurrence, and impact.

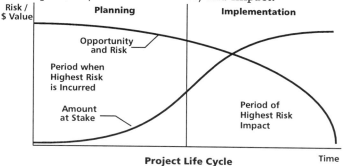

Figure IV-1 Risk Versus Amount at Stake (R.M. Wideman, 1991)

The potential problem is not harmful and does not produce loss until it moves into the occurrence phase or the impact phase. The occurrence is a risk problem that is no longer potential but is in progress. Risk occurrences generally are categorized into two general types: risks that can be eliminated or minimized by using pre-planning techniques and risks that are unpredictable surprise situations solved by developing "fire-fighting" techniques. Potential problems and risk occurrences must be resolved by using problem-solving techniques.

The impact is the actual loss or harm to people, property, or other interests. Although the impact of risk occurrences can be minimized, it is assumed that such impacts are essentially final and irreversible. The degree of actual impact usually depends on management of the first two phases.

CATEGORIES OF RISK

Each risk development process falls into one of three categories.

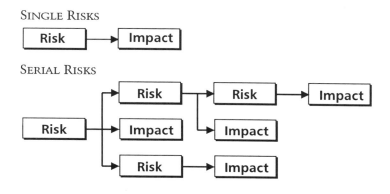

CONCURRENT RISKS

Single risks share such characteristics as that they usually occur over a defined period of time with a clear beginning and ending time. They can be described as single activities or events, as there usually are no other risk events occurring at the same time. Also, their impacts do not contribute to the development of other risk situations.

Serial risks develop from a progression of what might appear to be several risk events. However, instead of being independent of each other, each single event impacts other events, and they share some characteristics. For example, each of the events in a chain of reactions would not develop into an impact without the preceding events contributing to the impact. Also, the total impact of a serial risk is the combined effect of all the single impacts in the chain.

Concurrent risks are a combination of two or more independent single and/or serial risk situations that occur at the same time.

RISK ASSESSMENT FACTOR (RAF)

The risk assessment factor is a weighted product of probability and sensitivity used to compare evaluation criteria for probability and sensitivity. Probability is the potential that the risk will develop into an occurrence or impact. Sensitivity is the estimated magnitude of impact the risk would have if not addressed.

Risk Management

The risk management process is a formalized planning process that identifies both obvious and obscure risks. It provides a framework for identification, evaluation/implementation, and resolution of risk. Risk management is a process and a control system for project managers to formally identify risks and either accept or reject each risk, reduce its potential impact, or eliminate it altogether.

Risk management is implemented to avoid unnecessary impact costs, minimize crisis management, optimize utilization of limited resources, and appropriately transfer risks. Self-insuring risks are part of risk management.

Risk management involves the preparation of a risk management plan (RMP) involving a problem-solving methodology constituting a systematic approach based on the usage of multiple resources. Also, it is an iterative process, divided into the following steps:

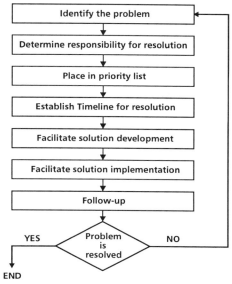

For each risk problem, a specific problem-solving theory should be applied. Risk problem-solving theories include the analytical approach, the intuitive approach, or a combination of both.

The analytical theory involves the solution of a problem through mathematical, scientific, or engineering principles (sensitivity analysis, probability analysis, Monte Carlo simulation, and decision tree analysis, for example). Most risk problems that involve too many variables cannot be solved through the analytical theory.

The intuitive theory includes the use of value engineering and life-cycle costing principles. It is based on rational problem-solving theories, experience, accumulated knowledge, and practicality (brainstorming, Delphi method, and decision theory). One very efficient method is the elimination process that very quickly narrows possible solutions.

To successfully control risk, a single individual should be responsible for conducting and monitoring all steps of the problem-solving methodology.

RISK MANAGEMENT PLAN

The objectives of a risk management plan include providing comprehensive documentation, risk identification process, and a control system composed of control schedules, a risk control system, and documentation control and reporting. There are four distinct stages in the development of the risk management plan. The first stage is the planning stage that occurs

---

before any commitments have been made to implement the project. The second stage is the analysis stage, which is implemented just before starting development. The third stage is the implementation stage that takes place in the beginning of the project's implementation, and the last stage is the maintenance stage, which involves the follow up and maintenance of the plan throughout the project.

The planning stage consists of identifying and analyzing all major risks associated with the project. This step can be combined with the function analysis workshop. The goal at this stage is not to identify every project risk but rather to determine if the project is desirable or if it should be fundamentally reviewed.

The analysis stage involves the identification, prioritization, and evaluation of risk pertaining to the development of the project. It should be combined with the concept stage value analysis workshop since it requires creativity, evaluation, and development of risk avoidance or mitigation proposals. This step can be repeated before implementation of the project.

During the first two steps, the goal is to eliminate risks or modify the project in order to avoid them by early identification and proactive problem-solving. Those two steps are team-oriented and, therefore, subject to integration with value management. Risks may be unrecognized, unmanaged, or ignored by default, but once they are recognized, a course of action must be set by the team to control them. Some examples for how to tackle a risk include the following: no action taken (voluntarily absorbed); avoided (by taking appropriate steps); reduced (by alternate approach); shared (joint venture, association); transferred (insurance, contract); retained and absorbed (contingency, allowance); or any combination of the above.

The third and fourth steps concern the risks that cannot be avoided and have to be resolved and are more specifically related to individual investigation by the risk manager.

The implementation stage consists of analyzing all previous risk information and conducting a detailed analysis of the entire project. This procedure will enable the project manager to adjust strategy, planning, and control systems to eliminate or minimize risk impact early in implementation.

The maintenance stage concerns the actual dealing with type I and type II risk impacts. If the three preceding stages have been performed well, this stage should be a relatively easy task to accomplish for the risk manager.

PROJECT ORGANIZATION
Project organization addresses the roles and responsibilities of key participants and delineates the reporting structure and communication

guidelines. It is an important part of the establishment of a risk management plan because it identifies the individuals who will be responsible for accomplishing tasks related to risk management.

PROJECT RISK ASSESSMENT MATRIX (PRAM)

The project risk assessment matrix (PRAM) reviews areas of risk and classifies risks according to risk groups, risk elements, and risk problems. It identifies potential risk problems by the project delivery phase, also. Known potential areas of risk include ability/experience of business/project management; quantity, quality, time, and cost; and design and implementation services.

Ability/experience of management includes the following potential risk areas: organizational structure, leadership ability, contracts, communications, compatible program and budget, adequate work load, team members, professional attitudes, management information and control systems (MICS), problem-solving methodology, and self-protection mechanisms.

CONTROL SCHEDULES

Control schedules used for risk management are the project control schedule, otherwise known as a "what-if?" schedule, and the risk control schedule, a potential risk blow-up

RISK CONTROL SYSTEM

The risk control system includes a risk control index list, a project risk analysis summary report, a priority analysis status report, and a risk analysis worksheet. It provides a consecutive listing of key identified risks, a summary of the risk resolution, and a record of the project delivery phase during which the risk was identified.

REPORTS/SHEETS

The **project risk analysis summary report** provides a summary of key information from priority analysis status reports, a risk priority number, and risk interdependencies. It also provides risk priority, estimated date of impact, and a record of the progress of risk resolution.

The **risk analysis worksheet** provides a record of the ongoing analysis of the risk, from its inception to its completion.

Benefits of Risk Management

Risk management is an essential function of project management; therefore, it is beneficial to include risk identification and analysis procedures in the value management process. Benefits of this procedure include: opportunities for minimizing impact costs, increased possibility of achievement for project completion, lower occurrence of quality defects, better control of scope deviation, optimization of resource utilization, and overall added value.

Quality Modeling

Quality is directly related to performance. If a product works exactly as designed and expected, it is considered a high-quality product.

Alphonse Dell'Isola
Fellow, SAVE International

Dr. Stephen J. Kirk, vice president of Smith, Hinchman & Grylls (SH&G), presented quality modeling at the 1994 Society of American Value Engineers conference. This method of analyzing customer quality expectations and managing quality over the life-cycle of a project is very simple and effective. Although the presentation focused on construction projects, this method is readily adaptable to other types of projects; only the quality model elements would have to change accordingly. The following section is an edited transcript of Dr. Kirk's presentation.

Introduction

Modeling, measuring, and managing quality are critical to meeting owner expectations regarding the planning, design, and construction of their facilities. The approach presented is based on total quality management (TQM) and consists of three parts: modeling quality expectations, measuring quality conformance, and managing project quality.

Our experience has shown that this approach is equally applicable to all types of facilities including financial, health care, industrial, research and development, and corporate office facilities.

Modeling Quality Expectations

The quality model is the entry point during the planning phase for establishing and developing the owner's project criteria. In an interactive workshop setting, project expectations are identified, explored, and documented. These expectations may involve schedule, image, flexibility, functionality, technical systems performance, budget adherence, or any other issue that may shape the direction of the project. The relative importance between these competing values are explored, prioritized, and documented with the owner.

The quality model provides a thorough definition of the project performance expectations required by the owner. SH&G has found that most project expectations can be organized into twelve competing value elements.

Through collaborative workshops with the owner, a clear understanding, documentation, and prioritization of the above competing values are realized for the project. These expectations and goals are explored and discussed in the workshop. Specific owner definitions of each competing value are developed. The quality model consists of narrative descriptions of each value and a graphic diagram that shows the relative priorities between the twelve major competing values.

For each element of the quality model, up to six components may vary depending on the project type. For example, the components of "operational effectiveness" for a health care facility might include average length of stay, staff cross-training efficiency, appropriate functional adjacencies, just-in-time supplies delivery, staffing ratio/patient/treatment/visit, and "right sizing" (square feet/functional area).

For an industrial facility, the operational effectiveness components might include production rate, maximized utilization of equipment, minimized process travel distances, just-in-time supplies delivery, staff hours/unit of production, and square feet/unit of production.

Element:

Engineering Performance	Quality Scale

Component:	Wt	Minimum Acceptable		Owner Expectation		Ideal Solution	
		0 1	2	3	4	5	6
Air Quality	50						
		Air Filtration 35% R.H. (summer): 50-60% R.H. (winter): No suppl. Outside air: 20 CFM/pers.		Air Filtration 65% R.H. (summer): 50-60% R.H. (winter): 25-30 % sup. Outside air: 20 CFM/pers.		Air Filtration 95% R.H. (summer): 50-60% R.H. (winter): 30% suppl. Outside air: >20 CFM/pers.	

Figure IV-2   Quality Measurement Scale

Figure IV-2 illustrates the quality measurement scale for the component "air quality" of the "engineering performance" element. These measurement scales are later used to evaluate alternatives as the project begins to move into the design phase.

The participants in the quality model workshop normally represent five points of view so that when a consensus decision is reached, all areas of interest have been addressed. These five types of participants include the owner (financial), user (functional use), designer (architects/engineers), builder/constructor, and facility manager (operations and maintenance).

This collaborative workshop environment involving the client and the analysis/engineering team helps to build a clear mutual understanding of objectives, how the facility should perform, what issues are the most important, and, most of all, what the client ultimately requires, both tangibly and intangibly.

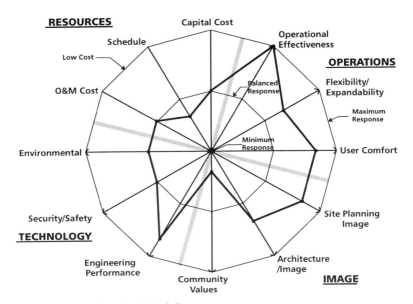

Figure IV-3   Quality Model

Figure IV-3 illustrates a quality model diagram for a new university science building. It represents the relative weighting of importance among the twelve quality elements. A low response indicates an element is less important than other elements. The weighting for each element is determined by consensus among those faculty members in attendance at the workshop on the campus. Following is an interpretation of the results shown in Figure IV-3.

Measuring Quality Conformance

Measuring quality begins during the design of the project; costs, for example, are normally estimated (measured) during the schematic, design development, and construction documents phase of design.

In a similar way, the other elements of the quality model are used to "measure" the project design for conformance. The measurement scales that were prepared during the quality modeling effort are used to assess how well the actual design meets the predefined "owner expectations." In some cases the design may not only meet the owner expectations but also may come close to achieving the "ideal solution" described on the quality component measurement scales. Other quality components may be only "minimally" satisfied by the actual design solution. The purpose of measuring quality is to determine if the design is conforming to the owner's original quality expectations. Just as with cost, if the design does not minimally achieve the quality objectives, management action is required to make adjustments.

Category:	Image							
Element:	Architectural Image							
		Minimum Acceptable		Owner Expectation		Ideal Solution		
Component:		1	2	3	4	5		
Residential Character	25					◯	125	
Non-institut. Image	25				◯		100	
Visual Interest (aged)	20			◯			60	
Historical Context	15				◯		60	
Inviting Outdoor Spcs	10			◯			30	
Enhanced Views	5			◯			15	
Total Weight	100					Element Score	390	

Figure IV-4   Element/Component Scores

Figure IV-4 illustrates the measurement of the element, "architectural image," for a health care facility located in an historic area of Washington, DC. The weighting, measurement, and resulting score are calculated based on the quality component measurement scales developed earlier. Other design alternatives also are measured using the same component scales.

Managing Project Quality

Managing project quality is achieved in part by holding a series of value engineering workshops that occur at each of the project design milestones including schematic, design development, and, occasionally, construction documents. This workshop approach permits team problem-solving and consensus. Participants also represent the five points of view described earlier.

During the three-to-five day value engineering workshop, participants creatively generate a wide variety of alternatives to enhance the project design in order to approach meeting the quality conformance expectations defined in the quality modeling effort. Study areas are selected based on the results of the quality conformance measuring effort. For example, if some space functional adjacencies were not achieved, resulting in reduced "operational effectiveness," then the value engineering team would explore alternate layouts to improve this quality component.

Lessons Learned

The value engineering technique of quality modeling is very useful in defining, measuring, and managing owner project quality expectations. Application of the quality modeling approach on a variety of facility types during the past four years has resulted in the following observations:

- The quality modeling process provides an opportunity for the owner's team to collaboratively establish project expectations involving members of differing perspectives.
- Quality modeling often identifies "issues" that would not have been otherwise discovered until late in the design and construction process.
- Left without a method for measuring conformance, building area typically increases 5 to 10 percent during the design process.
- Once a project is bid, area (gross square feet) reduction will only decrease costs by 50 percent of the bid dollars/gross square feet.
- Resolution of cost overruns does not always have to be managed by increasing scope.
- Without a method for measuring conformance, net to gross ratios tend to slip 5 to 10 percent during the design process.
- Undefined site components and building "special" foundation, architectural, mechanical, and electrical systems represent the largest risk to budgets.
- Design/build does not save money; it simply limits the contractor's risk by limiting the owner's options regarding project quality.
- Traditional project delivery methods that do not stress criteria development during the planning phase tend to define scope requirements through an iterative (and expensive) design process.
- Projects without a managed emphasis on meeting owner quality expectations during the design process do not achieve the best value for the project budget.

QUALITY MODEL ELEMENTS
OPERATIONS
Operational Effectiveness. The degree to which the building is able to respond to the work process and flow of people, equipment, and materials.

Flexibility/Expandability. The degree to which the building plan can be rearranged to conform to revised work processes and personnel changes. The ability of the building to grow to meet projected changes in the work process without disturbing existing building functions.

User Comfort. How the building provides a physically and psychologically comfortable place for people to work and live.

Capital Cost Effectiveness. The economic consequences of the building in terms of initial capital investment including construction cost, design fees, land costs, and so on.

Operations and Maintenance. The degree to which the building is able to conserve energy resources through construction, site orientation, and solar design. Other considerations include maintenance, operations, and replacement costs.

Schedule. The amount of time required to complete the various tasks including programming, design, construction, and start-up/move-in.

Environmental. The degree to which the facility is sensitive to environmental concerns such as hazardous waste, air and water pollution, use of sustainable materials, recycling, and so on.

Security/Safety. The degree to which the building can segregate sensitive functions from one another and prevent the entry of people to restricted areas.

Engineering Performance. How the building operates in terms of mechanical systems, electrical systems, and industrial processes.

Site Planning/Image. The degree to which the site responds to the needs of the project in terms of parking, vehicular and pedestrian traffic, outdoor amenities, and the visual impact to employees and visitors.

Architectural Image.

The visual concept of the building and the way in which the building attracts attention to itself. The form of the building and the degree to which it acts as a symbol for the company.

Community Values. How the building and its site project a "good neighbor" identity in terms of safety, security, and privacy.

Project Management

> *Value management cannot be divorced from the management of projects and provides a mechanism for integration to improve communication and information flows. This allows the exploration and interrelationship between time, cost, quality and function and any trade off between these.*

> John Kelly and Steven Male
> English Project Management Researchers

This section is an edited transcript of a paper entitled "Value-Added Project Management" that the author prepared for the 1996 International Project Management Association World Congress on Project Management.

Introduction

Lately, tighter budgets, higher exposure to scrutiny, and increased pressure by governmental and non-governmental organizations have resulted in even greater client involvement in projects and have led clients to request even more documented preliminary studies, design to cost (DTC), and fast-track execution in order to ensure the best response to the needs, shortest pay-back period, and highest return on investment. The manager's reputation is hanging on his capacity to deliver his client's project on time, on budget, and at the desired quality level.

In order to attain these goals, the project manager must acquire a better knowledge of all functions of a project much sooner in the project management process to aid in setting targets with more accuracy. This means that, with leaner budgets, clients are asking the project team to be more imaginative and creative and exercise control early in the project in order to stay within the fixed boundaries of the agreed upon scope. It is therefore of the utmost importance that the original budget and schedule be decided with the maximum measurable data and represent the actual needs of the client. The consequence of this premise is that the project manager needs to identify, as soon as possible and with maximum accuracy, the alternatives that will affect the project the least pertaining to scope, quality, and duration, as well as without adversely affecting the budget.

In his book, *Le rapport qualité/prix* (1985), Robert Tassinari states: "Value increases when the satisfaction of the Customer's need augments and the expenditure of resources diminishes." Value management is seeking the highest value for a product or project. By integrating value management techniques into the concept and development phases, it is possible to master the value of the project in a continuing operation where a certain number of workshops are used to define, analyze, and control that value.

In order to increase the net savings potential of management decisions, the project manager must include them as early as possible in the project, thus multiplying the risk factor associated with a high percentage of conjecture versus fact. When developing the project plan, assumptions often are made to fill gaps created by the lack of information. Value management—because of its function orientation accented by performance rather than solutions and its structured job plan and multi-disciplinary team work—helps complete early data with measurable and documented information.

As shown in Figure IV-5, the use of value management during project definition will increase the knowledge of the project and enable the project manager to gain lead time by allowing him or her to make decisions at an earlier date, based on a higher percentage of measurable data.

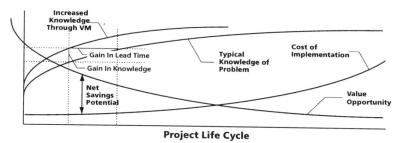

Figure IV-5   Potential Gains of Value Management Integration

Project Management Institute divides the project management practice into nine knowledge areas (Wideman 1991): four **core functions** (scope, quality, time, and cost) and four **facilitating functions** (human resources, procurement, risk, and communications) and **project integration management,** which consists of the development, execution, and control of the project plan.

The customer's need is defined through scope and quality; the expenditure of resources, through cost and time. Thus, the concept of "value" explicitly covers the four core functions; the use of value methodology enables their integration into a value system that also will encompass the four supporting functions and be incorporated into the project plan. The value system developed with this methodology will clarify goals and objectives, optimize evaluation of alternative solutions, and establish a consensus among all project participants.

Value analysis/engineering has traditionally been used as a "one shot" peer review exercise that has proven to create an adversarial relationship with the project team and impair the implementation of proposals. Lately, though, the tendency has been to work with the project team and spread the job plan into a series of workshops where output from one workshop is used as input for the next. Development is undertaken by participants between workshops. This latter method is the one that integrates the best within the project management process and is described in this book.

The methodology illustrated promotes the use of value management from project definition to project execution. Value management becomes the favored control tool of the project manager in the planning and development phases where you need a proactive and creative problem-solving method while all options are still open. Other control techniques can be used only when all parameters are set; value management will explicitly state the client's value system, covering all aspects of the project. The project manager will rely on the analytical aspect of functional analysis and value analysis in the first two phases and on the overall concept of value throughout the entire project in order to cover each project management core and supporting function.

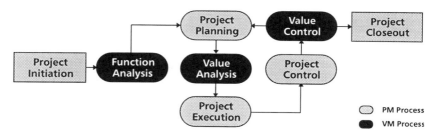

Figure IV-6   The Value Management Integration Process

We will now examine how value techniques will be integrated into the project management process to increase the overall project (product) value. The techniques described herein have all been implemented by the author in conjunction with project management, specifically during the project pre-design and design phases. The proposed methodology involves the application of the job plan over a certain period of time and within a number of workshops from the project start to its final design and execution.

Function Analysis

The only reason for extensive functional analysis is to correct our ignorance factor so we can see the project in its true light.

Thomas J. Snodgrass

Function analysis occurs during the initiation phase of the project; it is an integral part of the strategic planning and feasibility process. The first step with a project is to clearly identify the needs and objectives of the client and make them unequivocal for every participant in the project. The value team has to establish the actual functions (expected performance) of the project (product) with the client. Function analysis can be used effectively to determine the scope and environment of the project which will create a baseline for change management; it is the basis on which the program (brief) of the project will be built.

Partnering principles and the planning stage of risk management are included in this part of the value management integration process.

The Function Analysis Workshop (Step 1)

In the proposed methodology, the goal of the function analysis workshop (FAW) is to identify, compare, and classify the functions in order to build a function model of the project called a function breakdown structure (FBS).

It is essential that the participants in the workshop include representatives of the client involved with the project concept, development, execution, and use because needs and objectives should be defined and evaluated from every possible angle for the function breakdown structure to be endorsed by every participant.

Value Analysis

Once function analysis is completed, value analysis will be implemented to find the best alternatives needed to fulfill the identified functions by optimizing the resources (money, time, human, and material). It is during this phase of the process that the analysis stage of the risk management procedure should be integrated.

Value Analysis Workshop (Step 2)

A first value analysis workshop will be scheduled in the pre-design phase to clarify the client's needs and have the program (brief) validated by all participants under the guidance of the value analysis practitioner. It will cover the information, creative, and evaluation phases of the job plan. The development phase will be undertaken after the workshop by the designers, and the value analysis workshop report will be used as the baseline for the design. This workshop creates a strong bond between all participants and helps get the design team on the right track very quickly and efficiently by maximizing their knowledge of the project. Partnering, risk analysis, constructibility, procedures, and procurement issues should be addressed during this workshop to ensure covering the entire value system of the project.

Value Control

In order to cover all aspects of the client's needs when specific problems arise, control with a value perspective should be addressed throughout the course of the project.

Value Control Workshops (Steps 3 and 4)

At the end of the preliminary design, before the final design is approved, a mandatory value analysis workshop (step 3) is held to specifically address conformity to the program (brief). It will confirm scope compliance or deviation from baseline regarding quality, schedule, and cost and help generate quality alternatives for any changes in scope that have occurred due to unforeseen conditions, or bring the project back within original objectives. Using the input from previous workshops, the value control workshop should directly address the creative and judgment phases but only if the participants are the same as those who participated in the earlier workshops. Development of the proposals can be made outside of the workshop environment. At the conclusion of this workshop, the design team should be able to finalize its design and very quickly enter into the production of procurement documents.

At any time in the project life-cycle, in case of serious deviations from the project parameters, a targeted value workshop (step 4) will be held. The cause of the deviations should be quickly identified and addressed, and the workshop will require participation of only the stakeholders for that particular problem in order that it can be run quickly and efficiently. This is one case where it might be useful to bring in external design professionals to get a new perspective on the project.

Follow Up and Implementation

The project manager must be convinced that value management will enable delivery of a more customer-oriented project and lessen the risk associated with early decision-making. In order to obtain efficient value analysis proposal implementation, the project manager must obtain the consensus of all participants, especially the design team that will develop the proposals.

The project manager also must secure from the client an endorsement of the value analysis team proposals by convincing the client that the money she has spent is put to good use. The use of value management reports, including models and tables, will facilitate communication and understanding of the proposed solutions and reassure clients about the amount of control the project manager has on the project.

It should be remembered that the real success of value analysis will not be measured by the amount of proposals generated in the creative phase but by the success of proposal implementation.

Conclusion

The value management methodology ensures the customer that the end product (result) will correspond to his need. Also, by increasing the knowledge of the project and avoiding scope misinterpretation, it will save significant amounts of money due to budget and schedule overruns (unnecessary design or redesign fees, claims, loan interest, life-cycle costs, low return on investment, and longer pay-back period).

The methodology illustrated here covers most of the techniques used in large or complex construction projects. In smaller or simpler projects it is important to follow the framework of the method without necessarily entering into every detail of specific techniques. When value management integration is not possible, individual value analysis workshops can still prove to be a valuable control tool that can generate a return on investment from 5.1 to 20.1 percent.

Value management and project management integration in construction are promoted mostly by architects who are fluent in value management techniques. Their command of programming (briefing) and design have made them acutely aware of the importance of early project definition and control. Good examples of such people are Steven Kirk of Smith, Hinchman & Grylls (SH&G) in Detroit and Howard Ellegant of Howard Ellegant Associates in Chicago.

In the United Kingdom, J. Kelly and S. Male, English quantity surveyors, have extensively discussed and promoted value management in their book, *Value Management in Design and Construction* (1993). Construction projects like Bovis' Broadgate and Ludgate in London have demonstrated the power of value management integration. In Canada, firms such as Decarel have begun integrating value management into the project management process on such projects as the Montreal Casino with significant success.

Value management integration readily applies to other fields, such as civil works, high-technology research and development, software development, environmental services, organizational procedures, and reengineering, among others.

In order to derive maximum benefit from value management, organizations must implement it at both the strategic and tactical levels, which means that clients should accept that value is the ultimate goal in any project endeavor. It is very important—in order for value management to realize its full potential—that the client and project manager be convinced of the power of value management integration and obtain commitment from all the participants early in the project when no firm commitments have been made by any party. This will save costs in redesign fees, claims, and useless efforts.

When this course of action is implemented, it then becomes possible to enhance communications and team spirit, increase knowledge of the project to facilitate decision-making, achieve optimum overall performance with less resources, and generally improve projects and organizations, thus, creating **value-added project management**.

Appendix A

Value Management Associations

The following list was updated by the author at the time of publication. Some countries are indicated without naming an association because although the author is aware of the existence of a value association, he has not been able to obtain its address and/or references.

Australia
Institute of Value Management of Australia (IVMA)
The Secretary, IVMA, Level 15 McKell Building, Rawson Place, Sydney, Australia
Tel: +61 (0)2 9209 4143 Fax: +61 (0)2 9699 3148

Austria
Zentrum Wertanalyse im Wirtschaftsforderungsinstitut der Bundeskammer der Gewerblichen Wirtschaft

Belgium
Association pour le développement de l'analyse de la valeur (AVD) Founded: 1984
French: AVD c/o Fabrimetal, rue Puissant, 15 B-6000, Charleroi, Belgique
Tel: +32 71 44 54 41 Fax: +32 71 43 78 34
Dutch: AVD c/o F. Manas, Veritec, Desguinlei, 92, B-2018, Antwerpen, België
Tel/Fax: +32 3 238 79 15

Brazil
Associação Brazileria de engenharia e analise do valor

Canada
Canadian Society of Value Analysis (CSVA) Founded: 1993
Société canadienne d'analyse de la valeur (SCAV)
Attention: Pauline Marquis, 4970 place de la Savane, Montréal (Québec) H4P1Z6, Canada
Tel: +1 514 345 1655 Fax: +1 514 341 1216
E-mail: centreconstruction@mail.transc.com
Web site: http://www.scav-csva.org/ (French)
Web site: http://www.scav-csva.org/index2.html (English)

Denmark
No formal value management association; contact:
Danish Technological Institute (DTI)
DTI, Attention: Mr. Poul Pedersen, Gregersenvej, P.O. Box 141, DK-2630
Taastrup
Tel: +45 42 99 66 11 Fax: +45 42 99 54 36

France
Association française pour l'analyse de la valeur (AFAV)
Founded: 1978
Attention: M. Guy Quintaa, Tour Europe, Cedex 07, F.92049, Paris la
Défense, France
Tel: +33 (1) 42 91 60 45 Fax: +33 (1) 42 91 56 56

Germany
Verein Deutcher Ingenieure, Zentrum Wertanalyse (VDI ZWA)
Founded: 1974
Graf-Recke Straße 84, PostFach 10 11 39, D-40002 Düsseldorf, Deutchland
Tel: +49 (0) 211 62 14 426 Fax: +49 (0) 211 62 15 475

Greece
No formal value management association; contact:
Federation of Greek Industries

Hong Kong
Hong Kong Institute of Value Management (HKIVM)
Attention: Mr. Patrick Fong, Membership Secretary
c/o Department of Building and Real Estate, Hong Kong Polytechnic
University, Hung-Hom, Kowloon, Hong Kong
Tel: +39 2766 5801 Fax: +39 2764 5131
Web site: http://home.bre.polyu.edu.hk/~bsqpshen/hkivm.htm

Hungary
Society of Hungarian Value Analysis (SHVA) Founded: 1993

India
Society of Indian Value Management (SIVAM)
No. 906, II Main, IV Block, Rajajinagar, Bangalore—560 010
Tel: +91 805-35-0734/26-6599
Indian Value Engineering Society (INVEST) Founded: 1977
INVEST-EZC, Room No. 17, R.M.C.E., Jubilee Road, Circuit House East,
Jameshedpur—831 001
Tel: +91-657-424135, Attention: Mr. Ashok Pandit
Fax: +91-657-431209/431140/431160

Ireland
No formal value management association; national association due in 1997; contact:
The Learning Centre (FORBAIRT) Attention: Dudley Fowler
Glasnevin, Dublin 9, Ireland
Tel: +353 (0)1 808 2000 Fax: +353 (0)1 808 2020
E-mail: learning@forbairt.ie
Web site: http://www.forbairt.ie

Israel
No formal value management association; contact:
Israel Institute of Productivity

Italy
Associazione italiana per l'analisis del valore (AIAV)
Founded: 1985
Fondazione IDI, Via Larga, 31, 1-20122 Milano
Tel: +39 (0)2 92 102854 Fax: +39 (0)2 335694

Japan
Society of Japanese Value Engineers (SJVE) Founded 1965
c/o Kijoo Narasaki, SJVE INternational Liaison
E-mail: jdq03004@niftyserve.or.jp
Sun Building, 2-16-5 Jiyugaoka, Meguro-Ku, Tokyo 152, Japan
Tel: +81 (0)3-3724-9115 Fax: +81 (0)3-3724-6425
Web Site: http://www.sjve-hp.or.jp

Kuwait
No references available

Netherlands
(Workgroup, part of the Dutch Association of Cost Engineers)
Werkgroep Waarde Analyse (WWA of DACE) Founded: 1985
Vlietweg 14, Postbus 443, NL-2260 AK Leidschendam
Tel: +31 70 32 00 400 Fax: +31 70 32 03 903

Portugal
Associação Portugesa para a analise do valor (APAV)
Azinhaga dos Lameiros à estrada do Paço do Lumiar (edificio J), P-1699 Lisboa Codex
Tel: +351 (1) 758 9181 Fax: +351 (1) 758 9091

Russia
No references available

Saudi Arabia
No references available

South Africa
Value Engineering and Management Society of South Africa (VEMSSA)
Founded: 1977
Attention: Kurt J. Huber, International Liaison and Accreditation Chairman
P.O. Box 2963, Fourways, 2055, South Africa
Tel/Fax: +27 11 789 7163

South Korea
Society of Korea Value Engineering (SKVE)

Spain
Associación española de analisis del valor (ANAVA)
Founded: 1989
Attention: Ignacio Atorrasagasti, Paseo de la Castellana, 141, E-28046 Madrid,
España
Tel: +34 1 528 9345 Fax: +34 1 571 2831
Associación Catalana de Análisis des Valor (ACAV)
Founded: 1989
Via Layetana, 39, E-08003, Barcelona, España
Tel: +34 3 319 2300 Fax: +34 3 310 0681

United Kingdom
Institute of Value Management (IVM) (formerly **Value Engineering
Association**) Founded: 1966
Attention: Brian Mattingsley, 46 Passmore, Tinkers Bridge, Milton Keynes,
MK6 3DZ
Tel/Fax: +44 (0) 1908 234774

United States
SAVE International (formerly **Society of American Value Engineers**)
Founded: 1958
National Office, 60 Revere Drive/Suite 500, Northbrook, Illinois 60062
Tel: +1-312-480-1730 Fax: +1-312-480-9282
E-mail: value@value-eng.com
Website: http://www.value-eng.com

Appendix B

WWW Sites

Australia

Department of Public Works and Services, New South Wales
http://www.dpws.nsw.gov.au/vm1.html
Value management is concerned with assisting government to gain the best value for money in the development, procurement, and management of public infrastructure.

Department of Public Works and Services
http://www.dpws.nsw.gov/au/vm1.html
A simple site that defines the use of value management at the department.

Canada

Canadian Society of Value Analysis
http://www.scav-cvsa.org/index2.html
Founded in 1993, the CVSA is a non-profit organization that promotes value engineering as a means of improving companies' competitiveness. The site also is available in French: http://www.scav-csva.org/

ValuSoft Inc.—Value Engineering Software/Value Analysis Software
http://WWW.CAM.ORG/~vesoft/
A Canadian company that provides software to support the facilitator during a value engineering/analysis workshop. Downloading of software is available. The site also provdes links to other value management sites (http://WWW.CAM.ORG/~vesoft/links.htm)

Germany

Verein Deutche Ingenieure
http://www.wi-inf.uni-essen.de/~vdi/start.htm
Site in German, mostly engineering; consists of a webletter that sometimes contains information regarding value management in Germany.

Hong Kong

Hong Kong Institute of Value Management
http://home.bre.polyu.edu.hk/~bsqpshen/hkivm.htm
Home page of Hong Kong Institute of Value Management run by Dr. Geoffrey Shen of Hong Kong Polytechnic University. Not much information at present.

Ireland

Forbairt Learning Center
http://www.forbairt.ie/learning
Forbairt is a para-governmental organization that promotes innovation. Its learning center provides value management training leading to certification, following the German model.

United Kingdom

CIRIA value management publication:
http://www.mutelibtech.com/users/bm37/96-53.htm
Value management in construction: a client's guide. The guide also covers value engineering and shows how value management may be used to improve the overall value and performance of construction projects.

ICE Institute of Chartered Engineers, UK
http://www.ice.org.uk/ice/public/rf25-03.html
The situation of value management in the United Kingdom and a definition of its use, as viewed by United Kingdom engineers.

Value management—a quick guide:
http://www.dti.gov.uk/m90s/m9bd13001/m9bd130012.html
This booklet has been produced by the Department of Trade and Industry, United Kingdom (Central Government Department) as a guide for senior managers to value management.

University of Leeds—Value Management Group
http://www.leeds.ac.uk/civil/research/conman/value/value.htm
The site provides details of the group's research activities in value management and includes abstracts from its publications.

Value Management Research Group, The University of Reading
http://www.reading.ac.uk/~kcrsmstr
The site provides details of the group's research activities in value management and includes abstracts from its publications.

Design Procedures in Engineering
http://www.staffs.ac.uk/engs/des/aids/procedures/desvalan.htm
The Department of Engineering, Staffordshire University, explaining how value engineering can be used during the design phase of a product's life-span.

United States

SAVE International
http://www.value-eng.com/
Provides a series of links to other value management sites (http://www.value-eng.com/links.html) and value consultants list.

The American Government's Bureau of Reclamation
http://www.usbr.gov/valuprog
The site provides an overview of the bureau's value program used to comply with Public Law 104-106. Clear explanations are provided of how a value program should be implemented in an organization. Federal Transit Administration: http://www.fta.dot.gov/library/program/LL9.htm

The State of Massachusetts Highway Engineering Department
http://www.magnet.state.ma.us/mhd.mqi/valuee.htm
The page provides details of how value engineering is used in conjunction with other techniques to achieve the state's "quality initiative" (MQI) for its highway engineering program.

The United States Army Corp of Engineers
http://www.hq.usace.army.mil/cemp/e/ev/cemp_ev.htm
The page gives details of how the Corps of Engineers uses value engineering in its procurement process. Extracts are provided of the legislation controlling the use of value engineering by the Corp.

Washington State Value Engineering Innovation Project
http://www.wolfenet.com/~jhill/ve_main.html
In 1995 the 54th Washington State Legislature focused on improvement of the current value engineering process used by school districts for all school construction in Washington state. Details are provided of projects on which the improved value engineering process was used.

ValuLink—The Value Community's Home Page
http://libra.wcupa.edu:80/ValuLink/
An American page advocating the virtues of value engineering in cost reduction. Provides examples of projects on which value engineering has been implemented.

NASA
Value Engineering Bibliography
http://mijuno.larc.nasa.gov/dfc/biblio/vebiblio/html
Bibliography and definitions of value engineering, value analysis, and function analysis. Very well documented site with broad references.

Lawrence D. Miles Value Foundation
http://www.valuefoundation.org/
Contains interesting details about the life of Larry Miles, as well as some of his quotations. Also contains publications and bookstore, displaying a wide range of books on value.

Appendix C

Value Analysis Forms

LIST OF VALUE MANAGEMENT PROPOSALS (CREATIVITY)

ITEM	BRAINSTORMING PROPOSALS	COMMENT (EXPECTED VALUE IMPROVEMENT)	STATUS	ACTION
1				
2				
3				
4				
5				
6				
7				
8				
9				
10				
11				
12				
13				
14				
15				
16				
17				
18				
19				
20				
21				
22				
23				
24				
25				
26				
27				
28				
29				

Status: A-Accepted; R-Rejected; D-Develop

EVALUATION OF VALUE MANAGEMENT PROPOSALS

Value assessment: V: Better; 0: No change; X: Worse   Status A: Accepted; R: Rejected; D: Develop

No.	Proposal	Value assessment			Status	Comments	Action by
		Quality	Time	Cost			
1							
2							
3							
4							
5							
6							
7							
8							
9							
10							
11							
12							
13							
14							
15							
16							
17							
18							
19							
20							
21							
22							
23							
24							
25							

Note: Value criteria (quality, time, cost) can change according to study focus.

VALUE PROPOSAL DEVELOPMENT FORM

FUNCTION / ELEMENT	NAME OF PROJECT VALUE MANAGEMENT PROPOSAL				CHAMPION	STATUS	PROPOSAL NUMBER

PROPOSAL					VALUE ASSESSMENT

DESCRIPTION / ILLUSTRATION

COST EFFECT
Initial Costs
☐ Soft Costs
☐ Construction Costs
Product Life Costs
☐ Operation Costs
☐ Maintenance Costs
☐ End of Life Costs

TIME EFFECT   Weeks
☐ Design Time
☐ Construction Time
☐ Overall Time

QUALITY EFFECTS
☐ Producibility
☐ Usability
☐ Reliability
☐ Maintainability
☐ Availability
☐ Operability
☐ Flexibility
☐ Social Acceptability
☐ Affordability

COST CALCULATIONS	CURRENT	PROPOSAL	NET RESULT	ADVANTAGES	DISADVANTAGES	ACTION PLAN
INITIAL COST						Action By:
PRODUCT LIFE COSTS						Action Date: Notes:
TOTAL LCC COST						
TOTAL PRESENT VALUE						

Bovis Value Management *If needed, attach other sheets for additional information*
s:\bvm\projects\dublinrail\dub-vmp.ppt

Status Key: A = Adopt R = Reject F = Futu
Value Assessment: ✓ = Good ✗ = Bad

References

BOOKS AND ARTICLES

Adam, B. 1989. *Animer une étude analyse de la valeur: guide pratique des procédés et techniques efficaces*. ESF éditeur—Entreprise moderne d'édition—Librairies techniques, Paris, France.

Association francophone pour le management des projets. 1991. *Le management de projet, Principes et pratique (Collection Association française de normalisation (AFNOR) gestion)*. Paris, France: Association française de normalisation (AFNOR).

Akiyama, K. 1991. *Function Analysis: Systematic Improvement of Quality and Performance*. Cambridge: Productivity Press Inc.

American Society for Testing Materials (ASTM) Subcommittee E-06.81 on Building Economics. 1995. *Standard Practice for Performing Value Analysis (VA) of Buildings and Building Systems*, Standard Designation: E 1699-95. Philadelphia: American Society for Testing Materials (July).

Association française de normalisation (AFNOR), Commission de normalisation. 1985. *Analyse de la valeur, recommandations pour sa mise en oeuvre*, norme NF X 50-153. Paris: AFNOR (Mai).

———. 1990. *Analyse de la valeur, Caractéristiques fondamentales*, norme NF X 50-152. Paris: AFNOR (Août).

———. 1991. *Analyse de la valeur, Analyse fonctionnelle, Expression fonctionnelle du besoin et cahier des charges fonctionnel*, norme NF X 50-151. Paris: AFNOR (Décembre).

———. *Vocabulaire du Management de la Valeur, de l'Analyse de la Valeur et de l'Analyse Fonctionnelle, Partie 1: Analyse de la Valeur et Analyse Fonctionnelle*, norme NF EN 1325-1. Paris: AFNOR (Novembre).

———.1996. *Analyse fonctionnelle, Caracteristiques fondamentales*, norme NF X 50-100. Paris: AFNOR (Décembre).

Boulet, C. and J. Ballieu. 1995. *L'analyse de la valeur, collection "A savoir."* Paris: Association française de normalisation (AFNOR).

British Standard Institute. 1997. *Value Management,Value Analysis, Functional Analysis Vocabulary-Part I. Value Analysis and Functional Analysis*. BS EN 1325-1: 1997. London: BSI.

Brun, G. 1993. "Analyse fonctionnelle et le cahier des charges fonctionnel." Seminar, Montreal.

Bryant, J. W. 1986. "Customer oriented value engineering (COVE)." *Value World 9*, no. 1 (April/May/June).

Bureau of Indian Standards, Management, and Productivity Sectional Committee, EC 9. 1987. *Guidelines to Establish a Value Engineering Activity, IS: 11810-1986*, BIS, New Delhi, India.

Bytheway, C.W. 1985. "FAST diagramming." *Society of American Value Engineers Proceedings XX.*

———. 1992. "FAST—an intuitive thinking technique." *Society of American Value Engineers Proceedings XXVII.*

Charette, R.P. 1981. "The test reference building (TRB) concept for value engineering applications." *Society of American Value Engineers Proceedings XVI.*

Charette, R.P., and A. Shooner. 1995. "Increase VE team performance with the Uniformat II standard classification of building elements and related siteword." *Optimum V*, Canadian Value Analysis Society, Montreal.

Centre International des Grands Projets (CIGP) Project Management Terminology Committee. 1994. *Project Management Terminology (English-French)*, Montreal, Canada, Public Works and Government Services Canada, Office de la langue française, Gouvernement du Québec, International Center for Research and Training in Major Projects Management (CIGP).

Consell, D.G. 1992. "The European market for value analysis." Report. Luxembourg: Commission of the European Communities.

Construction Management Association of America, Inc. 1993. *Standard CM Services and Practice*, 2d ed., McLean, Va.: Construction Management Association of America, Inc. (CMAA).

Cook T. 1981. "Customer value." *Society of American Value Engineers Proceedings XVI.*

Cook T. F. 1986. "Determine value mis-match by measuring user/customer attitudes." *Society of American Value Engineers Proceedings XXI.*

de Bono, E. 1992. *Serious Creativity: Using the Power of Lateral Thinking to Create New Ideas.* New York: Harpers Business.

Delafolie, G. 1991. *Analyse de la valeur.* Paris: Hachette.

Dell'Isola, A. 1988. *Value Engineering in the Construction Industry.* 3d ed. Washington DC: Smith, Hinchman & Grylls.

Deutsche Industriell Normen. *Wertanalyse, DIN 69 910.* Germany: Deutshe Industriell Normen Institüt (Aug.).

Ellegant, H. 1993. "L'analyse fonctionnelle évite les pièges du TQM." *La Valeur n 56,* Association française de l'analyse de la valeur (AFAV), Paris, France (Avril).

———. 1993. "Modern value engineering: a proactive tool for project management." *The Project Manager* (Summer).

———. 1995. "Stop counting beans and start reducing surprises. pre-design VE for construction." *Society of American Value Engineers Proceedings XXX.*

European Commission, Directorate General XIII. 1995. *Value Management Handbook,* EUR16096 EN, ECSC-EC-EAEC. Brussels.

Fallon, C. 1965. "Using the combinex method in the measurement and comparison of value." *National Electronics Conference Proceedings XXI.*

———. 1977. *Value Analysis to Improve Productivity.* New York: John Wiley and Sons Inc.

———. 1980. *Value Analysis* (2d Revised Edition). Triangle Press.

Fowler, T. C. 1983. "The user oriented FAST diagram." *Society of American Value Engineers Proceedings XVIII.*

———. 1990. *Value Analysis in Design.* New York: Van Nostrand Reinhold.

Fuerstenberg, G.J. 1994. "Comparison of VE and TQM." *Value World* (Oct.).

Green, S. D. 1993. "A reinterpretation of value management." *CIB W-65, Organisation and Management of Construction—The Way.* Forward. Edited by T.M. Lewis. Trinidad, W. I. (Sept.).

Haviland, D.S. 1978. *Life Cycle Cost Analysis—Using It in Practice.* Washington DC: American Institute of Architects.

Hays, T. 1995. "Value analysis: the reengineering process." Canadian Value Analysis Society Symposium.

Her Majesty's (HM) Treasury, Central Unit on Procurement (CUP). 1996. *CUP Guidance Note No. 54 Value Management.* London: HM Treasury (Jan.).

Howard Ellegant Associates (HEA). 1986. "Value engineering for construction." HEA Brochure. Evanston, Il.

Ireland, L. R. 1991. *Quality Management for Projects and Programs.* Upper Darby, Pa.: Project Management Institute.

ISO Standards Committee. 1995. *Quality Management: Guidelines to Quality in Project Management (ISO/CD 10006 Committee Draft, Document: 176-2-8-N140)*, BSI, UK (March).

Kaufman, J. J. 1982. "Function analysis system technique (FAST) for management applications." *Value World* (July/September).

———. 1985. *Value Engineering for the Practitioner.* Raleigh: North Carolina State University.

———. 1992. Module I Workshop/Seminar, McGill University Management Institute, Montreal (Oct.).

Kelly, J., and S. Male. 1993. *Value Management in Design and Construction (The Economic Management of Projects).* London: E & FN Spon., Chapman and Hall.

Kirk, S. J. 1993. "Strategic value planning using VENTURE computer simulation modeling." *Society of American Value Engineers Proceedings XXVIII.*

———. 1994. "Quality modeling: defining project expectations." *Society of American Value Engineers Proceedings XXIX.*

Kirk, S. J., and K.F. Spreckelmeyer. 1993. *Enhancing Value in Design Decisions.* Detroit: Kirk and Spreckelmeyer.

MacPherson, S., J. Kelly, and S. Male. 1992. *The Briefing Process (A Review and Critique).* Edinburgh: Department of Building Engineering and Surveying, Herriot Watt University (June).

Miles, L. D. 1972. *Techniques of Value Analysis and Engineering.* 2d ed. New York: McGraw-Hill Book Company.

———. 1989. *Techniques of Value Analysis and Engineering.* 3d ed. Washington, D.C.: Lawrence D. Miles Value Foundation.

Mudge, A. E. 1971. *Value Engineering—A Systematic Approach.* New York: Mc-Graw Hill Book Co.

———. 1989. *Innovative Change, 101 Case Histories of Value Engineering.* Pittsburgh: J. Pohl Assoc.

Nakagami, Yoshio. 1994. "Present VE applications and potential needs in the Japanese industry." *Society of American Value Engineers Proceedings XXIX.*

———. 1994. "The status of VE application and management in Japanese industry." Paper presentation. 5th European Conference on Value Management (Oct. 6-7).

Order of Architects of Québec (OAQ) Architectural Practice Manual Committee. 1980. *Architectural Practice Manual.* Chapter 4.1, "The Architectural Project and its Phases." Montreal: OAQ.

———. 1989. *Architectural Practice Manual.* Chapter 4.4, "Programming." Montreal: (OAQ).

Osborn, A. F. 1971. *L'imagination constructive: comment tirer parti de ses idées.* 2d ed. Paris: Dunod.

Papageorge, T. E. 1988. *Risk Management for Building Professionals.* Kingston, Ma.: R.S.Means Co., Inc.

Parker, D. E. 1994. *Management Application of Value Engineering.* The Lawrence D. Miles Value Foundation.

Parker, D. E., and A. Dell'Isola. 1991. *Project Budgeting for Buildings.* New York: Van Nostrand Reinhold.

Peña W., S. Parshall, and K. Kelly. 1987. *Problem Seeking (An Architectural Programming Primer).* 3d ed. Washington, DC: American Institute of Architects Press.

Petitdemange, C. 1985. *La maîtrise de la valeur - conception, développement, qualité et compétitivité d'un produit.* Paris: Association française de normalisation (AFNOR).

———. 1995. *Analyse de la valeur et ing/nierie simultanee, collection "A savoir."* Paris: Association française de mornalistaiton (AFNOR).

Project Management Institute Standards Committee. *The Project Management Body of Knowledge (PMBOK).* 1987. Drexel Hill, Pa.: Project Management Institute.

———. 1996. *A Guide to the Project Management Body of Knowledge (PMBOK Guide).* Drexel Hill, Pa.: Project Management Institute.

Ravenne, C. 1989. *L'analyse de la valeur—Guide pratique pour les agents de maîtrise et techniciens.* Paris: Entreprise moderne d'édition.

Ruskin, A. M. 1995. "Managing design to cost engineering projects." *Project Management Journal* (Sept.).

Sandberg, H. R. 1983. "Evaluation." *Society of American Value Engineers Proceedings XVIII.*

Senge, P. M. 1990. *The Fifth Discipline—The Art & Practice of The Learning Organization.* New York: Currency Doubleday.

Sievert, R. W., Jr. 1991. "A review of value engineering as an effective system for planning building projects." *Project Management Journal* (March).

Smith, Hinchman & Grylls Associates Inc. (SH&G). 1993. "Value engineering application in the design & construction of facilities."

Module I, ACEC/American Institute of Architects Value Engineering Seminar/Workshop, Detroit, Mi.

———. 1995. "Project budgeting for buildings." Seminar, Montreal (Feb.).

Snodgrass, T. J. 1993. "Function analysis and quality management." *Society of American Value Engineers Proceedings XXVIII.*

Snodgrass, T.J., and T.C. Fowler. 1972. "Customer-oriented FAST diagramming." *Society of American Value Engineers,* Section 9.0.

Snodgrass, T., and M. Kasi. 1986. *Function Analysis—The Stepping Stones to Good Value.* Madison, Wi.: Board of Regents, University of Wisconsin System.

Society of American Value Engineers (SAVE). 1993. *Certification Examination Study Guide*, Northbrook, Il.: SAVE (May).

Stafford, D. H. 1995. "The judgment phase—more than one way to skin a cat." Module II Seminar by John Bryant, Certified Value Specialist, Montreal (April).

Tassinari, R. 1985. *Le rapport qualité/ prix*. Paris: Les éditions d'organisation.

———. 1987. *Conception pour un coût objectif—CCO (Design To Cost—DTC)*. Paris: Stage de formation, Association française pour l'analyse de la valeur (AFAV), Association française de normalisation (AFNOR).

———. 1992. *Pratique de l'analyse fonctionnelle*. Paris: Dunod.

———. 1995. *L'analyse de la valeur, collection "A savoir."* Paris: Association française de normalisation (AFNOR).

Thiry, M. 1996. "Value-added project management." Paper Presentation. International Project Management Association World Congress Project Management, Paris.

Wideman, R.M. 1991. *A Framework for Project and Program Management Integration (The PMBOK Handbook Series-Volume No.1)*. Drexel Hill, Pa.: Project Management Institute.

———. 1992. *Project and Program Management Risk Management, A Guide to Managing Project Risks and Opportunities, (The PMBOK Handbook Series-Volume No.6)*. Drexel Hill, Pa.: Project Management Institute.

Zimmerman, L. W., and G.D. Hart. 1982. *Value Engineering (A Practical Approach for Owners, Designers and Contractors)*. New York: Van Nostrand Reinhold Ltd.

VIDEOGRAPHY

Barker, J. A., and R.Y. Christensen. *The Business of Paradigms—Discovering The Future Series*. Bornsville, Minn.: ChartHouse International Learning Corporation, 1994 (38 min.).

Brethen, R. *Keeping the Competitive Edge With Value Analysis*. Phillips Industries (18 min.).

Copperman W. / **North Carolina State University**. *The Contractual Aspects of Value Engineering*. Northbrook, Il.: Society of American Value Engineers, 1985 (4 x 45 min.).

CRM Productions Inc. *Creative Problem Solving: How to Get Better Ideas*. New York: Mc-Graw-Hill, 1979 (25 min.).

Kaufman, J. J. / **North Carolina State University**. *Value Engineering—A Course for Education and Profession Development*. Northbrook, Il.: Society of American Value Engineers, 1985 (14 x 45 @ 55 min.).

Lawrence D. Miles Foundation. *Principles of Value Analysis/ Value Engineering*. Northbrook, Il.: Society of American Value Engineers, 1995 (34 min.).

Lawrence D. Miles Foundation / **North Carolina State University**. *The Story of Value Analysis*. Northbrook, Il.: Society of American Value Engineers, 1995.

Salenger Educational Media. *Creativity: The Only Way to Fly*. Santa Monica, Ca.: Salenger Educational Media Inc., 1983, (7 min.).

Society of American Value Engineers. *Value: The Success Criterion*. Northbrook, Il.: Society of American Value Engineers (12 min.).

ABOUT THE AUTHOR

Michel Thiry has more than twenty years of experience in construction as an architect and project manager. He has been practicing value management for more than five years and has obtained his certified value specialist certification from SAVE International (formerly Society of American Value Engineers) and recently obtained his certified value manager certification from the Institute of Value Management, United Kingdom. He is a registered project management professional with the Project Management Institute, has been awarded a "gold seal " certificate as project manager in general contracting by the Canadian Construction Association and membership with the Association for Project Management, United Kingdom). He also is a licensed architect in Québec (Canada) and New York (United States) and is a member of the American Institute of Architects.

During his career in Canada, he has been involved as an architect or project manager on such projects as the Montreal Convention Center, the Montreal World Trade Center and Inter-Continental Hotel, and the Quebec City Area and Montreal Casinos. While head of design management at the City of Montréal, he supervised the first value studies conducted on projects for the City. He presently works as a value manager for Bovis Program Management in the United Kingdom, which is part of the worldwide Bovis Group. He has conducted value studies on a wide range of projects including construction, water treatment, pharmaceutical, and transportation. He is currently responsible for developing the value management module for the Bovis Group self development program.

He recently has been admitted to Birkbeck College (University of London), the United Kingdom's leading department in organizational psychology, to pursue a master of science degree in organizational behavior.

He was founding vice-president of the Canadian Value Analysis Society 1993–1994 and has been secretary of the PMI-Montreal Chapter from 1994 to 1996. He was local coordinator for the Project Management Professional Committee that participated in the project management "Step-by-Step" cd-rom, launched at the Boston '96 PMI Symposium-Seminar. He was a regular instructor for the Project Management Professional Certification Examination Preparation Workshops held in Montreal and is currently involved in a training program for the Université Léonard de Vinci (Paris) in project and value management.

He has given numerous lectures at prominent conferences and written many articles for national magazines on the integration of value management into the project management process.